Jus

Just Joking

JUMBO

Contents

CHAPTER 1

Far-Out Space Silliness

HA!HA!HA!HA!
HA!HA!HA!
HA!HA!
HA!HA!

Q Why don't astronauts drink tea in space?

A Because the flying saucers are hard to hold on to.

pun FUN

The new **planetarium** got **stellar** reviews.

Q Why did the **cows travel** to space?

A They were following the Milky Way.

Did you know that **rhesus monkeys** have been sent on **space missions?**

The first two monkeys in space were named Albert I and Albert II.

ASTRONAUT: Waiter, I want to change my order.
WAITER: Is there something wrong with your salad?
ASTRONAUT: No, it's just that I'm craving something meteor tonight.

NATALIE: Where in space do you think the person meant when he said, "To boldly go where no man has gone before"?
KENDRICK: To use the bathroom in zero gravity.

Q

What's the biggest fashion statement in the galaxy?

A Orion's Belt.

MY STYLE IS OUT OF THIS WORLD!

TEACHER: Emily, did you do your solar system project for the science fair?
EMILY: Yes, of course. It was fantastic.

BURP!

TEACHER: What do you mean, "was"?
EMILY: A black hole ate it!

Q What's longer than a light-year?

A The first half of the school year.

Q Why was the astronomer surprised by her birthday party?

A She didn't planet.

HEATHER: Why did the astronaut take his two dogs on the space mission?
DWAYNE: Why?
HEATHER: So his pointer could spot aliens and his Labrador could retrieve them.

pun FUN

The cost of **creating** a human colony **on Mars** is **astronomical.**

Q Why was **Snow White** excited about the **space program?**

A She heard there were more than seven dwarf planets.

Q Why do aliens enjoy fairy tales so much?

A Because they start with, "Once upon a time in a land far, far away ..."

JERRY: What would you get if there were an ocean in space?
SARAH: Space waves?
JERRY: No, sea stars.

Q How do you take a dog into space?

A Crater!

OMESH: Do you think the New Horizons mission to Pluto will find anything?
ADRIAN: Probe-ably.

Ostriches, the world's largest birds, cannot fly.

KNOCK, KNOCK.

Who's there?
Radio.
Radio who?
Radio not, we're blasting off!

KNOCK,
KNOCK.

Who's there?
Eden.
Eden who?
Eden space ice cream won't give you a brain freeze.

Goats' eyes have rectangular pupils.

Q How does space stay clean?

A With meteor showers.

Q Why don't space boots have shoelaces?

A There would be too many astro-knots.

Q What did Neil Armstrong say when Michael Jackson did the moonwalk?

A Been there, done that.

Q How many balls of string would it take to reach the moon?

A Just one if it were long enough!

LAUGHABLE LIST

REJECTED NAMES FOR SPACE MISSIONS:

☐ Plan B ... or C ...
☐ The Lunatic Launch
☐ Budget Breaker
☐ Cross Your Fingers
☐ Here Goes Nothing!

MERCURY: You guys are just jealous because I'm the hottest planet in the galaxy!
JUPITER AND SATURN: We're the big players, though!
EARTH: Yeah, but I have all the life in this party!

TONGUE TWISTER!

Say this fast three times:

Stu's space suit suits Sue.

Q Which breed of dogs do aliens have as pets?

A Extra-terrier-estrials.

JOE: Why don't aliens eat clowns?
PETE: Their big shoes are hard to swallow?
JOE: No, because they taste funny.

13

SAY WHAT?

NAMES Galileo, Hubble, and Halley

FAVORITE ACTIVITY Staring up at the night sky from our treetops

FAVORITE TOY A telescope

PET PEEVE Cloudy nights

AN ASTRONAUT TOOK A BOOK TO READ ON HIS MISSION, BUT HE COULDN'T PUT IT DOWN!

I SAID GREAT APES NOT SPACE APES!

THE MOON LOOKS BROKE. IT MUST BE DOWN TO ITS LAST QUARTER.

IF SPACE IS A VACUUM, WHO CHANGES THE BAGS?

Adult male orangutans grow flappy cheek pads called flanges. Their faces have been likened to the man in the moon.

Why did the math teacher go to space?

Q Why haven't humans landed on Venus yet?

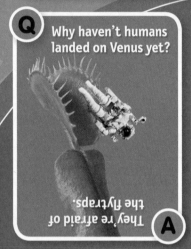

A They're afraid of the flytraps.

TEACHER: Hannah, your science paper is mostly blank. Where's the rest?

HANNAH: Oh, no, that's all of it. My topic was on the emptiness of deep space.

THE ISS IS A GIANT CAN OF TUNA, RIGHT?

Q What happened when the shooting star crashed to Earth?

A It was a dis-asteroid.

TONGUE TWISTER!

Say this fast three times:

Shipshape space shuttle.

SCIENCE TEACHER: A day on Venus lasts 5,832 hours. Can anyone think of something else that takes that long?
NATALIE: This lesson.

Did you know that, in 1963, French scientists sent the **first cat** to space?

Her name was Félicette, and her flight lasted about 15 minutes.

Q What does Saturn eat for dessert?

Moon pies. A

Q How do all the galaxies sing together?

In uni-verse. A

Q

What's Jupiter's favorite day of the week?

Moonday. A

THREE ALIENS CAME TO EARTH looking for the most powerful life-forms to show their leader.

The first presented a human and said, "This is found all over Earth and has the power to bring joy or sadness to those it encounters."

The second boasted, "I have the Internet. It dominates the attention of every human."

The third alien said, "My specimen can produce joy, sadness, and frustration. Humans serve it faithfully, it dominates the Internet, and it has more than one life."

"What is this amazing specimen?" the leader asked.

"A CAT," said the alien.

KNOCK, KNOCK.

Who's there?

Mars.

Mars who?

Mars-upials haven't been to space, but a lot of other animals have.

A game called the "Koala Space Program" was created for a NASA contest. In the game, these Australian marsupials "koalanize" Mars.

Say this fast three times:

Mick may cause crazy cosmic rays.

Q What do you call it when the moon photobombs Earth's selfie?

A A looney eclipse.

Q Why did the lady ask to buy the moon?

A She saw it was only a quarter.

CARLA: What do you call an alien with three eyes?
SUSIE: Scary?
CARLA: No, an aliiien.

BRIAN: Which celestial body is the smartest?
MARCUS: Earth, because it has all the scientists?
BRIAN: No, it's the sun, because it has the most degrees.

Q What did the astronaut say after a successful launch into space?

A "That was a blast!"

Q How can you tell you've found a love letter from space?

A It's signed X.O. Planet.

TOM: If there's a man in the moon, are there women in space?
EVA: Of course. The gal-axies.

pun FUN

When the space station called for an emergency fix, the astronaut was **a man on a mission.**

KNOCK, KNOCK.

Who's there?

Eclipse.

Eclipse who?

Me. The barber eclipse my hair too short every time!

Some elephant seals dive deeper than most submarines.

Q What happens when you get lost in space?

A You feel alienated.

TONGUE TWISTER!

Say this fast three times:

Surely the sun will shine.

Q What has spots, barks, and plays fetch in outer space?

A A Dal-martian.

pun **FUN**

The idea that the universe goes on forever **is way over our heads.**

KATHY: Did you hear that scientists have found life on another planet?
DANNY: Finally! Aliens on Mars?
KATHY: No, fleas on Pluto.

Q What kinds of **songs** do **planets sing?**

A Nep-tunes.

LAUGHABLE LIST

ASTRONAUT
FOOD CHECKLIST:

☐ Lunar-fish sandwiches
☐ Flying cup and saucer
☐ Unidentified frying objects
☐ Moon rocky-road ice cream
☐ Space jam sandwich
☐ Gravi-tea bags
☐ Astro-nuts
☐ Meteor loaf

Q What did the **star** name its **new puppy?**

A Sunspot.

Q How do you get a baby astronaut to sleep?

A You rocket.

23

pun FUN

Gravity is a real downer.

Q What do you call the dwarf planet Makemake if a meteor totally destroys it?

A Donedone.

BUZZ ALDRIN HAS TO BEE THE BEST ASTRONAUT NAME!

GAVIN: Who is the most active on social media?
WHITNEY: Celebrities?
GAVIN: No, NASA. It's always looking for stuff to comet on.

Q What's more impressive than doing the **moonwalk?**

A Performing a space walk.

Q Where do astronauts work on DIY projects?

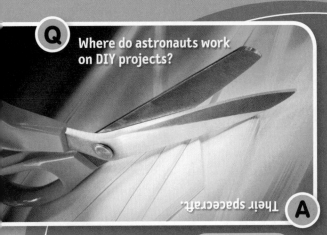

A Their spacecraft.

Did you know that 3,000 **honeybees** flew on the *Challenger* space **shuttle mission?**

Despite being in zero gravity, they made honeycombs just like they do on Earth.

TONGUE TWISTER!

Say this fast three times:

Shawn's schnauzer saw shooting stars.

Q Why does the
moon go
around
Earth?

A Because it can't go through it!

MICK: What do you call it when an alien comes face-to-face with an ostrich?
ELSA: What?
MICK: Close Encounters of the Bird Kind.

THAT'S ONE FUZZY EGG!

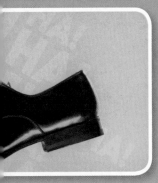

I WOULD DO ANYTHING TO GET TO OTTER SPACE.

KNOCK, KNOCK.

Who's there?
Gibbous.
Gibbous who?
Gibbous a telescope so we can see the moon better.

DID YOU KNOW THAT PLANETS LIKE TO READ NOTHING OTTER THAN COMET BOOKS?

An otter can hold its breath underwater for eight minutes—the same time it takes light from the sun to reach Earth.

"Zebra stripes" is a term used by scientists to describe stripelike features in Earth's magnetic field.

KNOCK, KNOCK.

Who's there?
Luke.
Luke who?
Luke, a shooting star!

Say this fast three times:

Rex wrecks red rockets.

Q What do dog astronauts say to mission control?

A "Beam me up, Scottie!"

Getting into the **asteroid belt** is a cinch.

Q What did the astronaut order at the diner?

A The launch special.

Q What happens when a rocket launch takes so long that people fall asleep?

A Instead of a liftoff, it's a drift-off.

DUSTIN: How well can aliens defend themselves if astronauts invade their planet?
KORA: Pretty well. They practice Martian arts.

Q What did **Mars** say when astronauts **landed on it?**

A "Ew, there's something crawling on my face."

Q What did the astronomer study in college?

A She ursa majored in physics and ursa minored in alien-outreach.

LAUGHABLE LIST

BUMPER STICKERS FOR THE INTERNATIONAL **SPACE STATION:**

☐ How's my orbiting? Call 1-800-TELL-NASA

☐ This Way Up?

☐ E.T. phone for pizza, with extra cheese, please!

☐ Honk if you love Zero Gravity

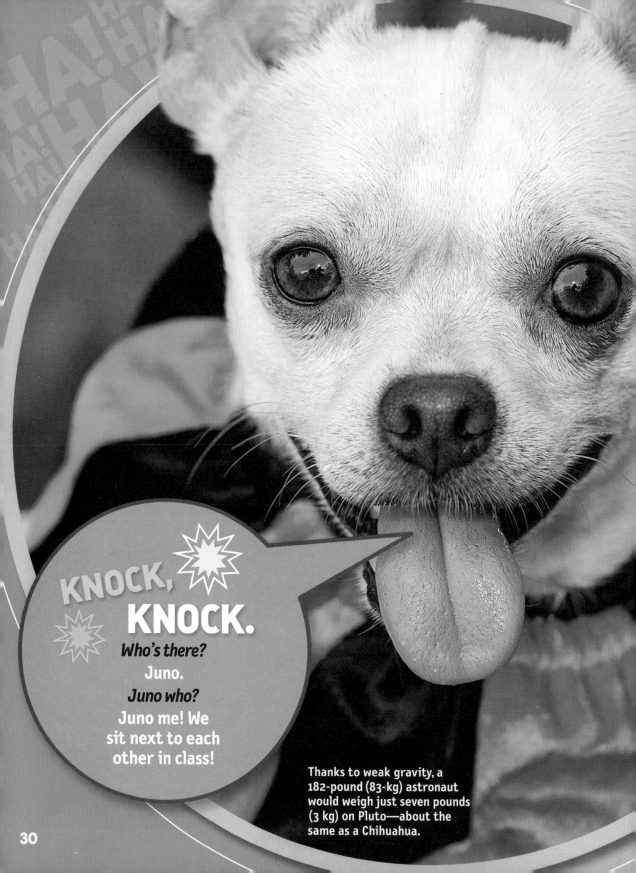

KNOCK, KNOCK.

KNOCK.

Who's there?
Juno.
Juno who?
Juno me! We sit next to each other in class!

Thanks to weak gravity, a 182-pound (83-kg) astronaut would weigh just seven pounds (3 kg) on Pluto—about the same as a Chihuahua.

Q

What holds the sun up in the sky?

A Sunbeams.

Q What did the runner-up at the Space Race win?

A A constellation prize.

TONGUE TWISTER!

Say this fast three times:

Yuri viewed the truly rural world.

Q How is Saturn like an old tree?

A Both have a lot of rings.

Q Why did the astronaut fail the exam?

A She spaced out and forgot the answers.

LAUGHABLE LIST

REAL VERSUS FAKE SPACE ACRONYMS:

- ☐ **ISS:** International Space Station vs. Important Silver Something-or-other

- ☐ **NASA:** National Aeronautics and Space Administration vs. Nice Aliens Should Apply

- ☐ **JSC:** Johnson Space Center vs. Just Seeking Cosmonauts

- ☐ **EVA:** Extra Vehicular Activity vs. Exciting Views of Aliens

Q

What did the alien order for dessert?

A A float.

SUN: What's up with your moon?
EARTH: What do you mean?
SUN: It's always turning it's back on me.
EARTH: Oh, sorry. It's going through a phase.

Q What do you call a magician in a UFO?

A A flying sorcerer.

LOL

SPACE

...accidentally
...d the
...footage showing
...NKIND'S FIRST
...the moon.

...ut
...s fellow

...the
...al
...E
...ON

ASTRONAUT Scott Kelly's identical twin, Mark, fooled NASA into thinking he was Scott at a mission launch.

WHOOPS!

When blasting off from the moon in 1969, THE EAGLE MODULE knocked over THE AMERICAN FLAG the astronauts had planted.

TWO ASTRONAUTS ONCE PRANKED A PIZZERIA ON APRIL FOOL'S DAY BY ORDERING A PIZZA DELIVERY TO SPACE.

DID SOMEONE ORDER A MOON PIE?

PIZZA

CHAPTER 2

Hilarious History

Q Who is a rodent's favorite philosopher?

A Soc-rat-es.

History knows how to make a comeback.

Q What does a **mummy** movie director say after the **final take?**

A "It's a wrap!"

Q What did the people do after establishing the Ottoman Empire?

A They put their feet up and relaxed.

Say this fast three times:

Madame Dame reigns in Spain.

Q Why did Vincent van Gogh decide to paint wheat fields?

A Because the photos he took were grainy.

Q Why wasn't the airplane invented before 1903?

A It required the Wright people for the job.

MARTY: If only I had been born 1,000 years ago.
TEACHER: Why?
MARTY: My homework would be so much shorter.

APRIL: Did you know that Christopher Columbus was in an a cappella group?
RENEE: No! When did that happen?
APRIL: After he hit the high seas.

Q Why were King Arthur's knights at the round table?

A Because his couch only sat three.

CHRIS: The queen pardoned the royal comedian even though his jokes weren't funny.
OLIVER: What did the royal court think?
CHRIS: That it was a nice jester.

Did you know that **King Louis XIV of France** wore wigs to hide his baldness?

He also wore high-heeled shoes, because he was short.

HAIR-RAISING, I KNOW!

Q What did the knight say when he accidentally fell off his horse?

A "Joust joking!"

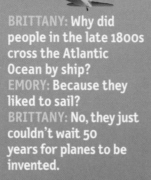

BRITTANY: Why did people in the late 1800s cross the Atlantic Ocean by ship?
EMORY: Because they liked to sail?
BRITTANY: No, they just couldn't wait 50 years for planes to be invented.

Q Which ancient Romans enjoyed their work?

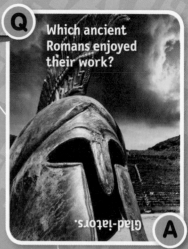

A Glad-iators.

Q What did the chicken say when asked who its favorite classical musician was?

A "Bach, Bach, Bach!"

Q Why did Louis XIV always want to play checkers?

A Because he loved shouting, "King me."

VALYNCIA: Which animals have the most royalty in their family?
KELSEY: Lions?
VALYNCIA: No, penguins, because there are royals, emperors, and kings.

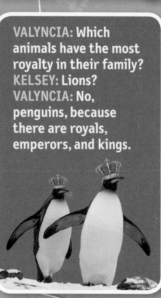

pun FUN

Some sculptures end up a bust.

JONAH: Who was the president with the most laundry?
ALISHA: Washing-a-ton.

Q Who is a pig's favorite historical figure?

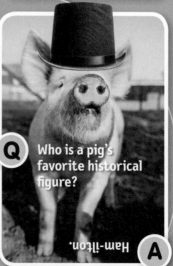

A Ham-ilton.

Two-million-year-old tiger fossils have been found in China.

KNOCK, KNOCK.

Who's there?

Khan.

Khan who?

Khan you tell me another history joke?

KNOCK,
KNOCK.

Who's there?

Noah.

Noah who?

Noah boat dock
around here?

Caimans are direct
descendants of dinosaurs.
They look the same today as
they did 65 million years ago.

Q What is a lion's favorite decade in history?

A The Roaring Twenties.

TEACHER: Why was Camelot important?
STUDENT: Back then it was the only place where you could find something to take you across the desert.

Q What's the name of the fearsome conqueror who was always getting confused?

A Attila the Huh?

Q What happened to those who lived during the Iron Age?

A They now rust in peace.

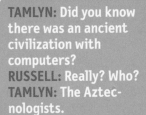

Q What did our prehistoric ancestors use to make extra-large sweaters?

A Woolly mammoths.

ROMAN TEACHER: Brutus, why are you late for class?
BRUTUS: Sorry. It toga long time to walk here.

TAMLYN: Did you know there was an ancient civilization with computers?
RUSSELL: Really? Who?
TAMLYN: The Aztec-nologists.

Q Why did the king have trouble breathing?

A He had no heir.

LAUGHABLE LIST

WEIRDEST JOBS IN HISTORY:

- ☐ Noah's ark-itect
- ☐ Camel-train driver
- ☐ Turkish-carpet fitter
- ☐ Car Mecca-nic
- ☐ Luxor-y hotel manager
- ☐ Ataturk-ey farmer
- ☐ Marco Polo shirt designer
- ☐ Petrified forest ranger

SAY WHAT?

NAME Sir Screech

FAVORITE ACTIVITY
Hanging out with other knight owls

FAVORITE TOY
Fancy-dress suit of armor

PET PEEVE
When the visor on my helmet slips and I'm left totally in the dark

THE BEST MAGICIAN IN HISTORY WAS HOO-DINI.

HISTORY WAS OWL-WAYS MY FAVORITE SUBJECT!

In ancient Greece, owls were symbols of wisdom. In medieval Europe, however, they were associated with witches.

CALL ME OWL-FASHIONED, BUT I LIKE A GOOD YARN.

HISTORY'S A HOOT!

KNOCK, KNOCK.

Who's there?

Manny.

Manny who?

Manny years ago they didn't have so much history to learn!

TEACHER: Who can tell us something about the Bronze Age?
DAKOTA: Everyone was a third-place winner.

Q Why is the United Kingdom such a damp place?

A Because there's been constant reign there for centuries.

Q What did the Egyptian pharaoh say when his adviser suggested hiring someone to take notes?

NOW HIRING

A "Hire-a-glyph!"

Q What did the British Empire have in common with ants?

A Colonies!

Q Why couldn't the two **navigators** ever agree on a direction to **sail?**

A Their personalities didn't Magellan well.

SHHH! KEEP IT UNDER YOUR HAT.

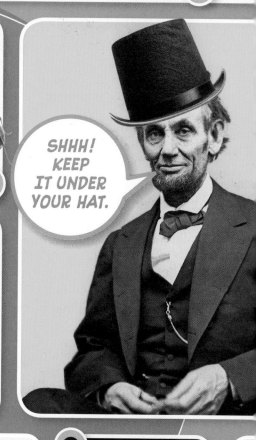

JESSE: Archimedes was a famous inventor and great mathematician, but he's better known for something else today.
DORA: What's that?
JESSE: Geometry homework! Without him, it wouldn't exist.

Q Why was Catherine the Great called that?

MEH!

A Because it sounds a lot better than Catherine the So-So.

Q How did Genghis Khan create the Mongol Empire, the largest empire in the world, during the Middle Ages?

YOU CAN DO IT!

With a Khan-do attitude, of course.

A

Did you know that U.S. president **Abraham Lincoln** kept important papers inside his hat?

The style of hat was called a "stovepipe" and was traditionally seven to eight inches (18–20 cm) tall.

TONGUE TWISTER!

Say this fast three times:

The duke drank a drop of dewdrop brew.

JOHANNES GUTENBERG: Ta-da! I created the world's first printing press! The movable type will make production easier, so we can make thousands of books! PUBLISHER: What, no autocorrect?

pun FUN

The president could full-Fillmore Grants, **but Congress** Hayes **been** Nixon them.

45

CHELSEA WHEELED A BIG, clunky machine **into class. It had two TV screens, a keyboard, and antennas sticking out on many sides.**

Chelsea pressed a big, red button and the machine hummed to life. Its lights, in various sizes and colors, illuminated the faces of her peers as they stared forward.

Chelsea announced, "For my year-end project, I built a time machine." "Wow!" the class gasped. "You could watch the pyramids being built in Egypt!" shouted Susie.

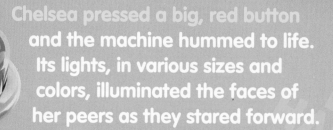

"You could see if we find aliens in the future!" beamed Ronnie.

"So Chelsea, if it really does work, what have you been using your time machine for?" her history teacher asked. "Well, my brother never believes anything I say," Chelsea said.

"Now I just bring back my future-self who says,

"I told you so!"

LAUGHABLE LIST

IF HISTORICAL FIGURES HAD EMAIL ADDRESSES:

☐ Cleopatra: QueenCatluver@PtolemaicDynasty.org

☐ Julius Caesar: RomanDude13@CoolRulers.net

☐ Charlemagne: HolyRomanEmperor1@CharlieTheGreat.com

☐ René Descartes: CogitoErgoSum@iam.net

☐ Vlad the Terrible: ChillinLikeAVillian@HouseofBasarab.org

Q Why did so many men want to work for King Arthur?

A They were in it for the knight life.

Q What was the name of the Egyptian ruler who always felt gassy?

A King Toot.

CAVEMAN OG: I've been taking art classes. I painted this one of us and the hairy beast we ate for dinner.
CAVEMAN BOR: That looks like an octopus driving a school bus.
CAVEMAN OG: What's an octopus?

pun FUN

No one's drawn a **conclusion** from the **Nasca Lines.**

Q Who's the most respected horseman in history?

A Paul Revered.

TONGUE TWISTER!

Say this fast three times:

Bartleby and Blake blew bugles.

Q Why did Edgar Allan Poe write poetry?

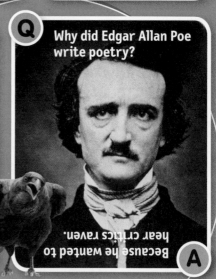

A Because he wanted to hear critics raven.

48

KNOCK, KNOCK.

Who's there?
Mayan.
Mayan who?
Mayan-truding?
I hope not.

Some ancient cultures mummified their Chihuahuas, believing that these little dogs helped their owners travel safely to the afterlife.

49

KNOCK, KNOCK.
Who's there?
Viking.
Viking who?
Viking requests ye come forth at once.

The laughing kookaburra's call has appeared in many movies; it's used as a substitute for the sound of a group of monkeys.

Q What did Henry VIII's doctor call him?

A Henry, he ate ... too much!

ANTONI VAN LEEUWENHOEK: Wow! I just discovered bacteria! High five!
FRIEND: Not until you wash your hands.

CARLY: Before the *Book of Kells*, there was another Irish masterpiece in the works, but it stank.
MORGAN: What was it?
CARLY: *Book of Smells*.

Q What did the American pioneers think while they were traveling to the West?
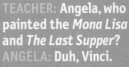
A This place is a-maize-ing!

Q Why were kings and queens so happy?

A Everywhere they went there was a royal party.

TEACHER: Angela, who painted the *Mona Lisa* and *The Last Supper*?
ANGELA: Duh, Vinci.

LUCY: Did you know Joan of Arc volunteered at a pet shelter?
JENN: Was she known as Joan of Arc then, too?
LUCY: No, she was Joan of Bark.

LAUGHABLE LIST

SEVEN BLUNDERS OF THE ANCIENT WORLD:

- ☐ Great Oval of Giza
- ☐ Hanging Socks of Babylon
- ☐ Statue of Zoot at Olympia
- ☐ Thimble of Artemis at Ephesus
- ☐ Mousetrap at Halicarnassus
- ☐ Colossus of Road Blocks
- ☐ Outhouse of Alexandria

Q How did the Vikings send secret letters?

A They used Norse code.

TEACHER: Does anyone know when the Dark Ages were?
PENNY: Yes, they were before we had smartphones.

An **archaeologist's** job is always **in ruins.**

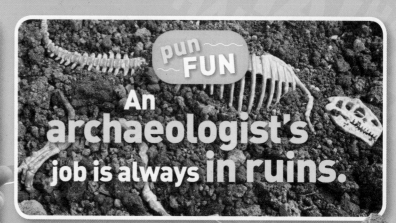

Q What kind of dreams did the Trojan horse have?

Nightmares. **A**

TOUR GUIDE: Long before the Great Pyramid of Giza, the Egyptians built another one that melted.
TOURIST: Really? What was it called?
TOUR GUIDE: The Great Pyramid of Cheese-a.

MMM. . . DELICIOUS!

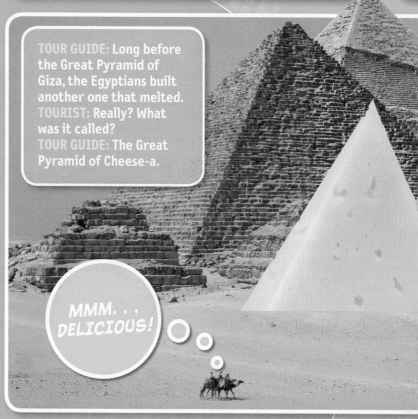

Q How did **William** the **Conqueror** get his **title?**

He took it. **A**

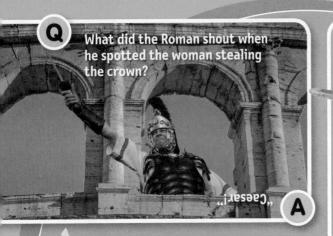

Q What did the Roman shout when he spotted the woman stealing the crown?

A "Caesar!"

Q Why was Alexander the Great called that?

A Because Alexander the Greatest Thing Since Sliced Bread wouldn't fit on his business card.

TONGUE TWISTER!

Say this fast three times:

Fix the sphinx, Phyllis!

KYLE: Did you see the movie about scientists who re-create giant prehistoric dogs?
LIZ: No, what's it called?
KYLE: *Jurassic Bark*, of course.

ART TEACHER: Cubism is the most important art movement in modern history.
STUDENT: Why?
ART TEACHER: Picas-I-said-so.

SAY WHAT?

MY COUSIN, THE ZEBRA, MUST BE THE WORLD'S OLDEST ANIMAL, BECAUSE IT COMES IN BLACK AND WHITE.

HISTORY IS AWESOME; I'M NOT FOALING AROUND!

WHO LIKES HISTORY? SAY YAY OR NEIGH!

Anyone could compete in a medieval tournament, as long as they had a horse, armor, a sword, and a shield.

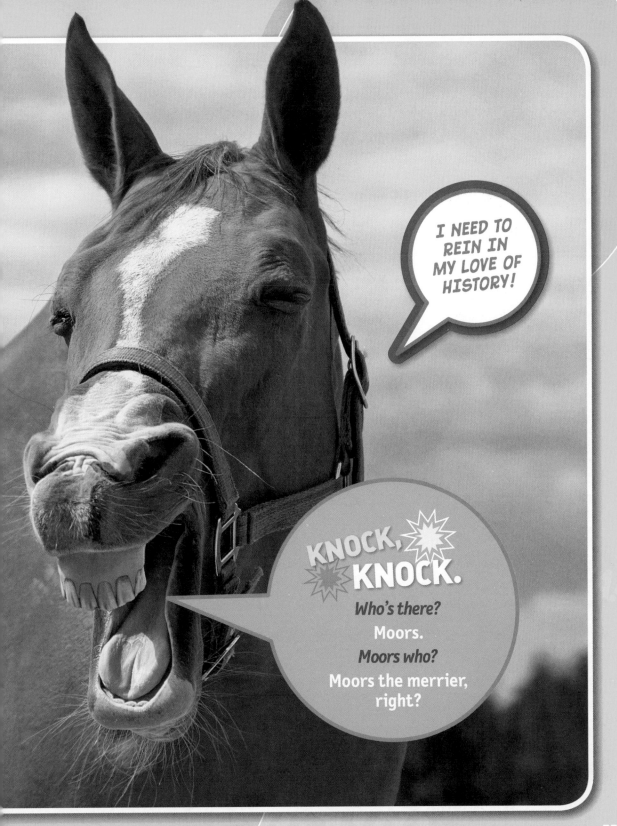

HISTORY TEACHER: Orson, when was the Battle of the Bulge fought?
ORSON: After Thanksgiving dinner!

Q What did John F. Kennedy say when he banged the car door into a fire hydrant?

"Oops, I presi-dent-ed it."

A

Q What kind of dog has a kingdom but no puppies of its own?

An heirless Chihuahua.

A

Q How did famous playwrights catch fish back in the day?

They Shakespeared them.

A

KIYOSHI: What do you call something that can take you back in time but makes you fall asleep in the process?
SHANNON: A time machine?
KIYOSHI: No, history class.

ALEXANDER GRAHAM BELL: Great news! I invented the telephone! Soon we'll be able to call each other up and share our feelings from anywhere in the world!
TEENAGER: Uh, there's no emoji keyboard? Lame.

Q How did Louis XIV come up with the name for his lavish palace?

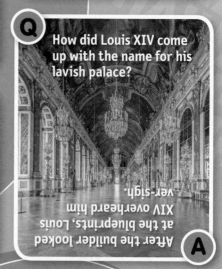

After the builder looked at the blueprints, Louis XIV overheard him ver-sigh.

A

pun FUN

History must be a **popular** subject, given **how many dates** it has.

56

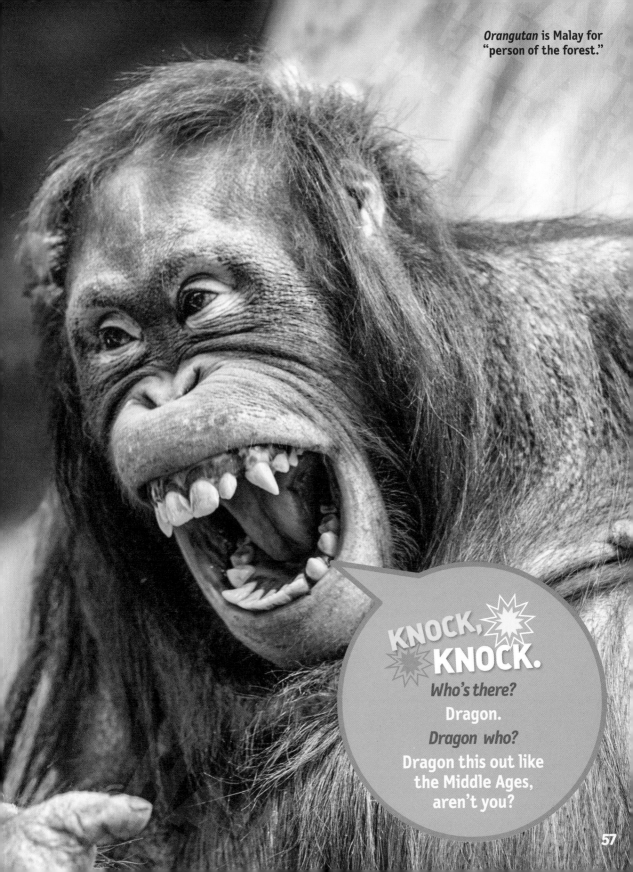

Orangutan is Malay for "person of the forest."

KNOCK, KNOCK.

Who's there?

Dragon.

Dragon who?

Dragon this out like the Middle Ages, aren't you?

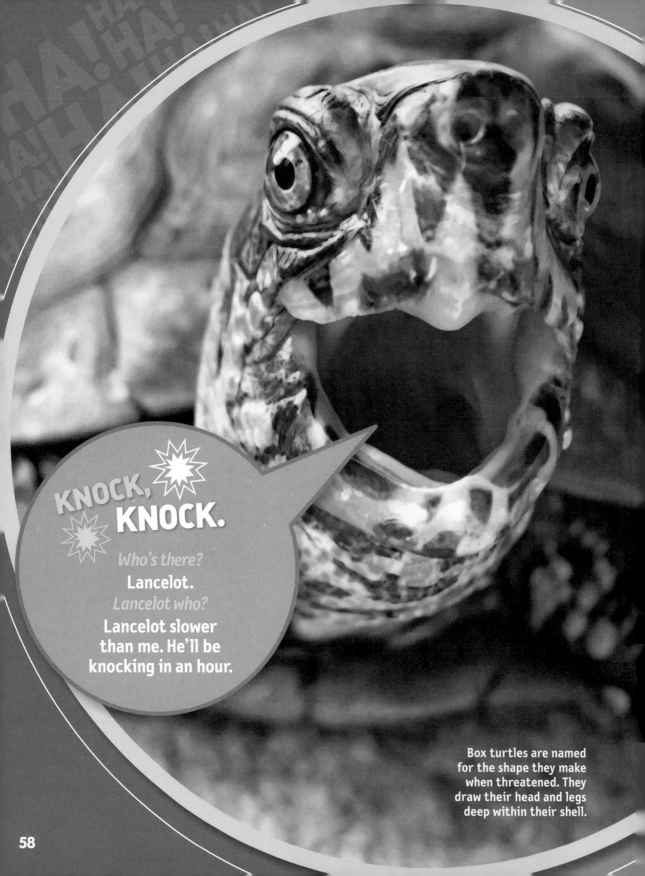

KNOCK, KNOCK.

Who's there?
Lancelot.
Lancelot who?
Lancelot slower than me. He'll be knocking in an hour.

Box turtles are named for the shape they make when threatened. They draw their head and legs deep within their shell.

Q Why did the king greet the people from a high balcony instead of on the street?

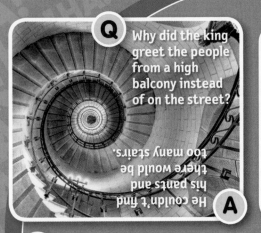

A He couldn't find his pants and there would be too many stairs.

TONGUE TWISTER!

Say this fast three times:

A brave bloke braids.

Q What did the Chinese say after the dynasty that ruled from A.D. 618–907?

A "Tang, that was a long time."

SETH: Do you know what Neil Armstrong said in 1969 when he walked on the moon?
CYNTHIA: No, what?
SETH: "That's one small step for man, one giant leap for space kangaroos."

Q Where did **cavemen** sleep?

A On bedrock.

PILGRIM #1: Do you think this new land will produce anything if we plant seeds here?
PILGRIM #2: It *Mayflower.*

Q What do you call the first rock climbers who got stuck?

A Cliff dwellers.

Q What was the name of the dog that ruled the animal kingdom?

A King Ar-fur.

LAUGHABLE LIST

OTHER NAMES
MARK TWAIN CONSIDERED FOR HUCKLEBERRY FINN:

☐ **Strawberry Trunk**
☐ **Blueberry Hoof**
☐ **Blackberry Ear**
☐ **Raspberry Beak**
☐ **Gooseberry Whisker**
☐ **Boysenberry Proboscis**

LOL HISTORY

The world's OLDEST recorded JOKE dates to 1900 B.C., and is about PASSING GAS.

THE WORD "JOKE" comes from the latin word IOCUS. And if the ROMANS thought something was SILLY, they said it was RIDICULOSUS!

MEDIEVAL COURT JESTERS used real dead chickens! Modern comedians use RUBBER CHICKENS—more yucks, less yucky!

KNOCK, KNOCK JOKES became popular in the 1920s.

WHAT'S THAT SMELL?

THERE IS A **GREEK JOKE BOOK** FROM THE FOURTH OR FIFTH CENTURY A.D. FILLED WITH MORE THAN **200 JOKES.**

CHAPTER 3

Comical Cuisine

KNOCK, KNOCK.

Who's there?

Pete.

Pete who?

Pete-za delivery!

Skunks are not fussy when it comes to food. They eat all kinds of insects, including bees and wasps. They eat venomous scorpions, spiders, and snakes, too, and are resistant to their toxins.

Say this
fast three times:

Boo drew blue blueberries.

NELSON: Did you hear about the chicken that applied for an office job?
JULIE: How did it go?
NELSON: At the interview the boss grilled him.

pun FUN

Popcorn jokes are corny.

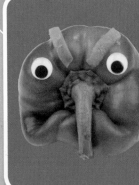

Q

What did one rabbit say to the other rabbits in the vegetable garden?

A "Turnip the beets and let's hip-hop!"

64

Q Why did the chef call a plumber?

A He spotted a leek in the kitchen.

Q What do you call an angry vegetable?

A Steamed.

ARIANA: Did you hear that a strawberry truck tipped over and spilled berries all over the highway yesterday?
RAY: Yikes! Was anyone hurt?
ARIANA: No, but cars were stuck in a jam for miles.

Q What did the police say when they caught the thieving cook?

LOOK AT THAT BERRY GO!

Did you know that **cranberries** are sometimes called **"bounce-berries"**? That's because when they are ripe they bounce like a **rubber ball.**

A "Don't move a mussel!"

Q How do professional chefs learn to cook so well?

A They wok hard to get butter every day.

Q How did the waiter announce that his Indian restaurant was running out of food?

A "Curry up or there will be naan left!"

Q What did the chef's parents say when they arrived at her restaurant without letting her know?

A "Soup-rise, we're here!"

DEVON: You shouldn't eat lunch next to your computer.
OLIVIA: Why not?
DEVON: Because it takes megabytes.

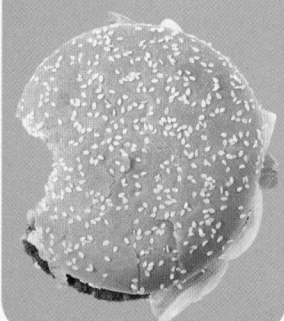

pun FUN

Ice-cream shops always have the scoop.

DAD: Fred, stop playing with your food.
FRED: But they're drumsticks!

Q What is a chef's favorite day of the week?

A Fry-day.

TONGUE TWISTER!

Say this fast three times:

Bits of butter better better the batter.

Q How do police catch food thieves?

A On steak-outs.

66

KNOCK, KNOCK.

Who's there?
Lettuce.
Lettuce who?
Lettuce in already!

Marmots are related to squirrels. They have huge front teeth for gnawing at plants. They also eat grain, insects, and worms.

Dolphins use their sharp teeth to catch prey, but swallow their food whole.

KNOCK, KNOCK.
Who's there?
Nacho.
Nacho who?
Nacho friendliest greeting, but hello to you, too!

Q How can you tell when the custard family is having a great day?

A They flan-t it.

Q What happened when the **onion** got a **paper cut** at school?

A The whole class cried.

Q Which type of grain is rarely seen?

A Uni-corn.

Q Why was the diner having a hard time eating dessert?

A It was pudding up a fight.

BIANCA: Where did Cinderella run into the butcher?
KIM: At the butcher shop?
BIANCA: No, at the meatball.

MIKE: Why do peppers have all the best gossip?
JORDAN: I don't know, why?
MIKE: Because they're jalapeño business.

pun FUN

A **baker's job** is a piece of **cake.**

Q What are dog biscuits made from?

A Collie-flour.

69

NAME Patch

FAVORITE ACTIVITY Chomping through bamboo...what else?

FAVORITE TOY Dominoes

PET PEEVE Interruptions to mealtimes

FEEDING TIME IN THE FOREST CAN BE PANDA-MONIUM!

PANDAS CAN HARDLY BEAR TO EAT ANYTHING BUT BAMBOO.

TEDDY BEARS NEVER GET HUNGRY BECAUSE THEY ARE STUFFED!

I'M FEELING BAMBOO-ZLED!

IS A BEAR WITH NO TEETH A GUMMY BEAR?

KNOCK, KNOCK.
Who's there?
Peas.
Peas who?
Peas be quiet!

Pandas eat as much as 36 pounds (16 kg) of bamboo a day— that's as heavy as 144 burgers.

Q Why are **potatoes** so popular on **social media?**

A Because of all the hashtags.

Q Why did the girl agree to go strawberry picking with her friends?

A She hoped to find berried treasure.

TONGUE TWISTER!

Say this fast three times:

Which sauce is fish sauce?

STOP! I CAN'T TAKE ANY S'MORE!

Q What did the maple syrup say after the all-you-can-eat brunch?

A "I feel waffle."

PASTA

CUSTOMER: Waiter, this alphabet soup doesn't look right.
WAITER: What's the problem?
CUSTOMER: Why, it's full of M pastas!

TONGUE TWISTER!

Say this fast three times:

Sherman's shrimp and chip shop.

72

Did you know that the **largest s'more** ever made weighed 267 pounds (121 kg)?

That's one-and-a-half times the weight of the **average adult** human.

HARPER: Do you want to eat German sausages or schnitzel for lunch?
LEVY: I'm not craving the wurst, so schnitzel do.

Q Why did the corn cancel at the last minute?

A Something popped up.

pun FUN

Potato recipes can be very a-peel-ing.

Q Why did the chef quit?

A His boss cut his celery.

Q How did the farmer react when her chickens suddenly laid golden eggs?

A She was shell-shocked.

73

It's a LONG story ...

AFTER MANY YEARS of entering different competitions, I found myself facing my first hot-dog eating contest.

My dad came to watch, and before the competition started, I told him I was really nervous. My last attempt at winning something had been at a spelling bee. I'd gotten myself in a jam, and my legs turned to jelly spelling the word "preserves."

He always had great advice so before the hot-dog eating contest, he said to me, "I can tell you what to do if you find yourself in a pickle and slipping behind everyone else."

I said, "Yes, please, what should I do?"

"Frankly, you'll just have to mustard the energy and ketchup!"

JOHN: Where did you learn how to make ice-cream desserts?
RACHEL: Sundae school.

Q What did the cows say after the farmer milked them?

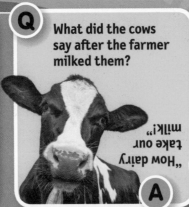

A "How dairy take our milk!"

Q What did the loaf of bread say when the bag broke?

A "When they see this, I'm going to be toast!"

Q Why did the bagel quit?

A It was tired of the hole thing.

Q What did the soda call its father?

A Pop.

SUNG: What is the cheapest kind of pasta?
LILY: What?
SUNG: Penne pasta.

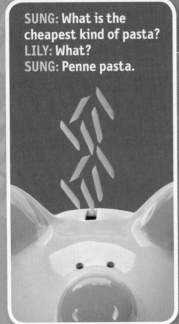

Q Where do you go to stock up on plates?

A The Great Wall of China.

Q What should you do with an onion when you're done with it?

A Ar-chive it.

76

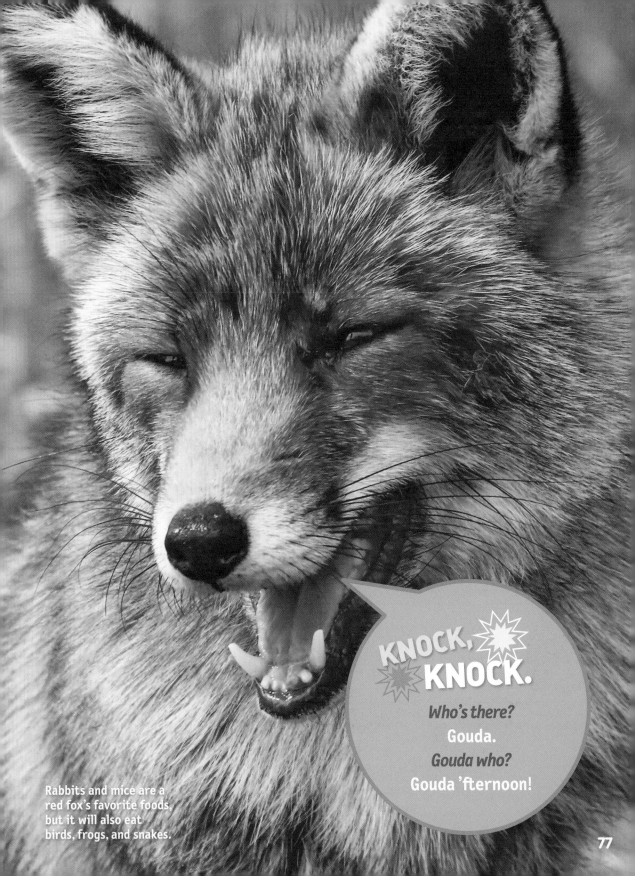

KNOCK, KNOCK.

Who's there?
Gouda.
Gouda who?
Gouda 'fternoon!

Rabbits and mice are a red fox's favorite foods, but it will also eat birds, frogs, and snakes.

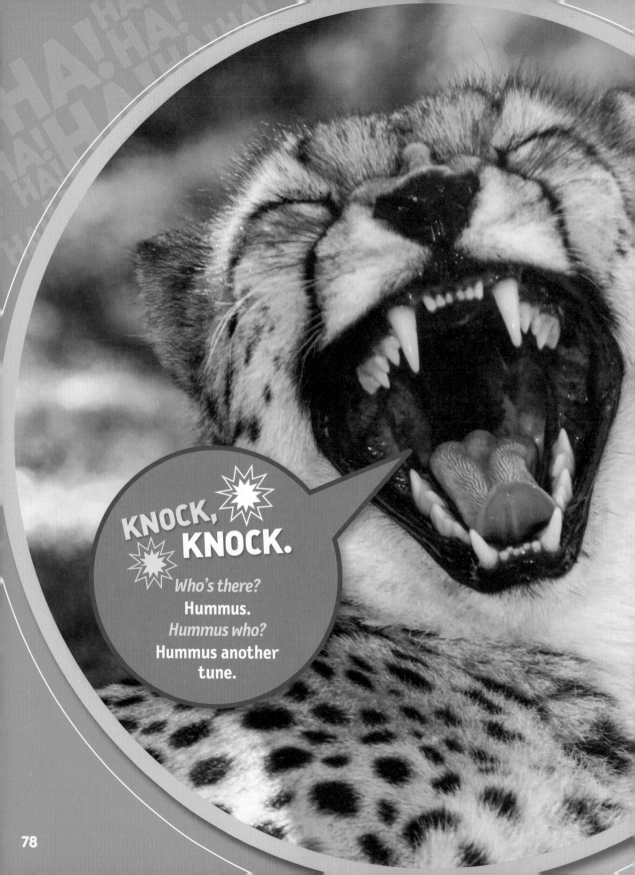

Q What did the small green fruit say after it was put in a pickle jar?

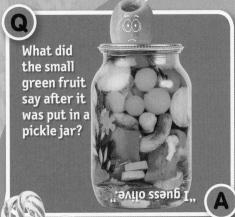

A "I guess olive."

pun FUN

Candy canes for sale—mint condition!

Q How does milk introduce itself in Spanish?

A "Soy milk."

Cheetahs can change direction in midair when chasing their prey.

Q How do you make a milkshake?

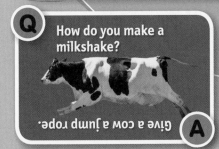

A Give a cow a jump rope.

Q How do you make gold soup?

A With 18 carrots.

LAUGHABLE LIST

HOMES ANTS WOULD LOVE TO EAT IN:

☐ Gingerbread house
☐ Ranch dressing
☐ Submarine sandwich
☐ Cottage cheese

TOBY: What do you get if you mix chutney with pickle?
WELSLEY: A mess!
TOBY: No, a good chuckle.

Q Why does the baker always have extra flour?

A He may knead it.

79

Q What did the waiter say when he spilled food on himself?

A "Dinner's on me tonight."

Q What did the fruit say when it was asked to go to the movies?

A "It's a date!"

TIME TO GET A NEW JOB!

SHERIFF: Can you describe what happened tonight?
HOT CHOCOLATE: Oh, it was terrible! I was mugged!

Q What does a baker use to
unlock her house?

A Coo-keys.

Q What happens during a food fight?

A Someone gets beef.

Q Which state is **always eating?**

A Massa-chew-setts.

Did you know that you can buy **octopus-flavored** ice cream in Japan?

You can buy eel-flavored soda, too!

CUSTOMER: Yuck! There's a bug in my salad!
WAITRESS: Peas romaine calm.

pun FUN

A **pickle** can be arrogant because it's a **big dill.**

SAY WHAT?

NAME Fluffy

FAVORITE ACTIVITY
Copying the way that mom and dad eat

FAVORITE TOY
My pond-side picnic set

PET PEEVE
When my pond ices over

KNOCK, KNOCK.

Who's there?

Soup.

Soup who?

Soup-er day outside!

DUCKS MUST GROW ON EGGPLANTS!

Some ducks have wide, flat beaks for feeding on plants, whereas others have narrow beaks for catching fish.

pun FUN

Lettuce is consistently ahead in life.

SOPHIA: How does a farmer mend his pants?
KENDRICK: I guess it must be when he sows!
SOPHIA: No, he covers the holes with little cabbage patches.

Q Why was the chocolate cake so flat?

A It had whipped cream and moose on top of it.

JODY: What does shredded cheese like least about school?
SANTOS: What?
JODY: Being grated.

EVALUATION
☑ Outstanding
☐ Very Good
☐ Satisfactory
☐ Marginal
☐ Unsatisfactory

Q What did the pancake say to the waffle?

A "Watch out for the knife. He'll try to butter you up!"

Q Why couldn't the **chef** make any **more pies?**

A He broke the mold.

TONGUE TWISTER!

Say this fast three times:

Patsy's perfect puff pastries.

Q What do you get when you mix chili peppers and hot bean soup in the blender but forget to put on the lid?

A A recipe for disaster.

LAUGHABLE LIST

SWEET AND SAVORY DISHES YOU MIGHT WANT TO SKIP:

☐ Banana split-pea soup

☐ Macaroni and cheesecake

☐ Shortbread and butter pickles

☐ Ice cream of mushroom soup

KNOCK, KNOCK.

Who's there?
Sherbet.
Sherbet who?
Sherbet day? I'm sorry I didn't bring a present.

Some macaques wash their food in salt water to give it more flavor.

85

Geckos are the only lizards that can vocalize to communicate. They chirp, bark, and click.

KNOCK, KNOCK.

Who's there?
Dish.
Dish who?
Dish better be what I ordered.

Q Why did the kids dress up as bread for school on Wednesday?

A It was for a roll-playing exercise.

Q How did the butcher introduce his **wife?**

A "Meat Patty."

ROBBIE: What do you get if you cross a bird with a kangaroo?
DEXTER: Do you get a spring chicken?
ROBBIE: No, you get pouched eggs.

Q What did the teacher say when the principal was eating all the pastries?

A "Donut eat the last one."

MARTIN: Have you had breakfast at the diner?
VICKI: No, how is it?
MARTIN: Eggs-cellent!

Q Why did the orange use suntan lotion?

A It didn't want to peel.

LAUGHABLE LIST

A CHEF'S TRAVEL ITINERARY:

☐ Week 1: Hungary
☐ Week 2: Cook Islands
☐ Week 3: Greece
☐ Week 4: Chile
☐ Week 5: Turkey
☐ Week 6: China
☐ Week 7: Iceland

CHARLOTTE: Which vegetables have the worst attitude?
GEORGE: I'm not sure, which do?
CHARLOTTE: Rude-abagas.

Q Who did Darth Vader summon when craving ice cream?

A Storm Scoopers.

87

LOL FOOD

A Japanese artist sculpts bananas into FUNNY-LOOKING FACES.

BANANA peels were considered SAFETY HAZARDS in 19th-century AMERICA.

There's a **restaurant** in BROOKLYN, **NEW YORK, U.S.A.,** that hosts **"silent meals"** —no laughing allowed!

Throwing a PIE in someone's **face is a gag that started** in SILENT FILMS.

THERE'S A **COMEDIAN** WHO SMASHES LETTUCE, WATERMELONS, AND EVEN BIRTHDAY CAKES ONSTAGE USING A TOOL CALLED THE **SLEDGE-O-MATIC.**

CHAPTER 4

Funny Bones

HA!HA!HA!HA!HA!HA!
HA!HA!HA!HA!
HA!HA!HA!

PUT YOUR HANDS IN THE AIR.

I WOULD IF I HAD ANY!

You are born with around 300 bones. Some are hard; others are made of a rubbery material called cartilage. The cartilage fuses with the bony bits as you grow, leaving you with 206 bones in all as an adult.

**Dr. Alice asks,
"Ankles
ail you?"**

pun
FUN

NEXT!!

Doctors need to have **patients.**

Q How did the mad scientist brainwash the townspeople?

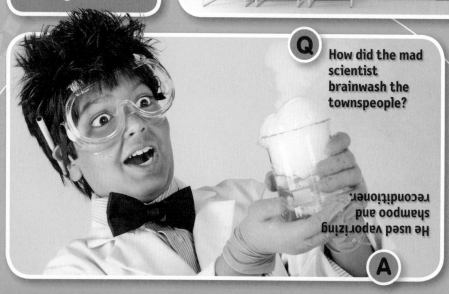

He used vaporizing shampoo and reconditioner.

A

Did you know that **chimps** are more closely related to **humans** than they are to **gorillas?**

Humans and chimps share more than 96 percent of the same genes.

DON: You know, we really shouldn't be afraid of sharks.
LUDO: Really? Why?
DON: Because they're totally armless!

CHLOE: Why are you holding a mouse under your nose?
DOMINIC: I always wanted to have a mouse-tache!

JAYDEN: There's a woman who can recite every part of the human body off the top of her head.
ALANA: Really? What's her name?
JAYDEN: Ana Tomy.

IT'S LIKE LOOKING IN A MIRROR.

Q What happened when the lady went scuba diving?

A She fell head over eels in love with it.

Q When can't your feet take you somewhere?

A When it's elbow room only.

Q How can **your face** tell when someone's **baking cookies?**

A It just nose.

Q Why was the girl only able to buy two things?

A Everything cost an arm and a leg.

SURGEON: Nurse, this looks worse than I thought. Call a cobbler!
NURSE: A cobbler? What's wrong?
SURGEON: The patient has a clog in her artery.

Q What do you call someone who stubs his toe?

A Howell.

CHRIS: Did you know there's another ear in addition to your right and left?
BECKY: Really? Where is it, then?
CHRIS: It's the frontier!

Q Why was the hair disappointed about the upcoming school play?

A It didn't get a part.

Q Why did the carpenter yell when he hit the nail?

A It was his thumbnail.

Q Why should you never fight a zombie?

A Because they'd happily eat a knuckle sandwich.

pun FUN

Sign language is definitely handy.

Q Why did the boy get a headache in math class?

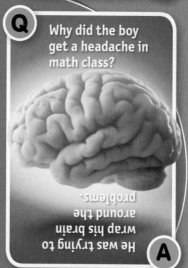

A He was trying to wrap his brain around the problems.

KNOCK, KNOCK.
Who's there?
Moustache.
Moustache who?
I moustache you to kindly let me use your bathroom.

A serval is a type of wildcat. Its big ears help it to hear the soft sounds of scurrying prey.

KNOCK, KNOCK.

Who's there?

Ewan.

Ewan who?

Ewan and I both have funny laughs.

A red panda wraps its tail around its body to keep warm on cold nights.

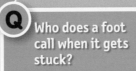
Q Who does a foot call when it gets stuck?

A A toe truck.

LAUGHABLE LIST

ANATOMICAL OCCUPATIONS:

- ☐ Navel officer
- ☐ Lumbar-jack
- ☐ Head chef
- ☐ Clavicle player
- ☐ Foot soldier
- ☐ Acupunctu-wrist
- ☐ Scalp-tor

pun FUN

Snowmen have sticky fingers.

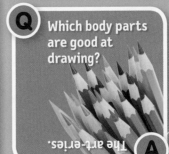
Q Which body parts are good at drawing?

A The art-eries.

MOM: Brad, today's a big day. You'll have to put your best foot forward.
BRAD: Oh, no.
MOM: What's wrong? If you keep standing there, you'll be late for your presentation.
BRAD: I can't move because I don't know which foot is better.

Q What is the hardest cold to fight?

A Kung flu.

Q Which part of your body never wins?

A De-feet.

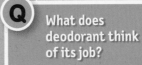
Q What does deodorant think of its job?

A It's the pits.

Q

SHHHH!

Why shouldn't you tell secrets in a cornfield?

A Because it's all ears.

Q Why did the zombie rip off his tuxedo and kick off his feet?

A He wanted to be footloose and fancy-free.

ANYONE KNOW A GOOD DENTIST?

TEACHER: Molly, why are you standing during the test?
MOLLY: Because you told us we need to be able to think on our feet.

Q What happened when the man lost all his hair?

A He bawled.

TONGUE TWISTER!

Say this fast three times:

Sherman shook soldiers' shoulders.

Q

How do **clowns** come up with their **material?**

A They use their funny bone.

Did you know that your **teeth** are as hard as a **shark's?**

A shark can grow and lose up to 30,000 teeth in its lifetime.

Q

Why did the **boy** bring a **ladder** to **class?**

A He wanted to be head and shoulders above the rest of the students.

pun FUN

When the **moustache dissed** the beard, it was a **sideburn.**

Q

Why did the **bride and groom** walk down the aisle on hot coals?

A So they wouldn't get cold feet.

A MAN WAS WALKING past a pet store when a bag of dog food fell off a delivery truck and landed on his head.

The heavy bag knocked the man out. The delivery truck driver quickly called for an ambulance, and the unconscious man was rushed to the emergency room.

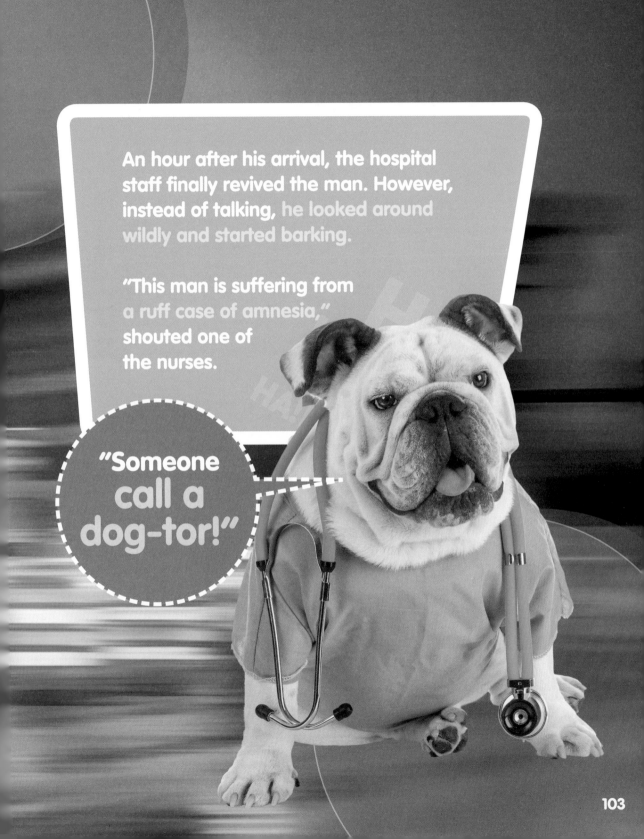

An hour after his arrival, the hospital staff finally revived the man. However, instead of talking, he looked around wildly and started barking.

"This man is suffering from a ruff case of amnesia," shouted one of the nurses.

"Someone call a dog-tor!"

KNOCK, KNOCK.

Who's there?
Albie.
Albie who?
Albie bright red
if I forget to
use sunscreen.

Although emus have
wings, they cannot fly.
They are fast runners,
though, reaching
speeds of 40 miles an
hour (64 km/h).

DOCTOR: If you exercise you won't get so many colds.
PATIENT: But my body is exercising, even right now.
DOCTOR: No it's not. You're just sitting in my chair.
PATIENT: But my nose has been running the entire time.

Q Why was the doctor laughing so hard?

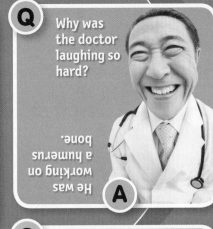

A He was working on a humerus bone.

Q When is a woman never hungry?

A When she carries a chip on her shoulder.

Q Why did the girl train her belly button to fight?

A To prepare it for navel warfare.

Q Where does the music in a hair salon come from?

A Headbands.

Q How is your dad like a lion when he sleeps?

A Because he sn-roars really loudly!

ALYSSA: Did you hear about the actress who kicked the entrance to the theater and got her leg stuck?
BEN: Oh, no. Is she okay?
ALYSSA: Yes, actually, she's very happy.
BEN: Why's that?
ALYSSA: Because she finally got her foot in the door.

pun FUN

Ghosts have uplifting spirits.

105

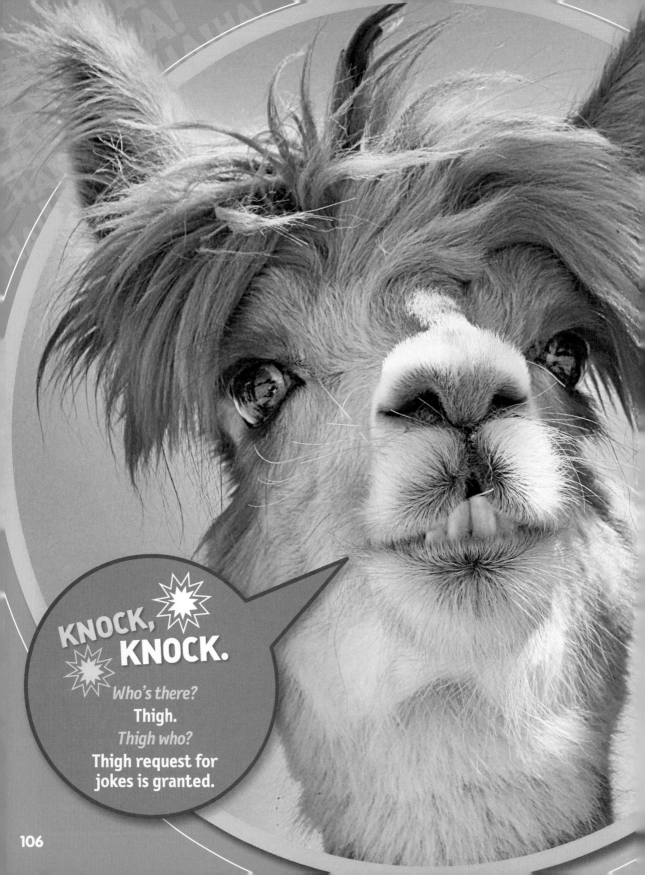

KNOCK, KNOCK.
Who's there?
Thigh.
Thigh who?
Thigh request for jokes is granted.

Q When is a hand a foot?

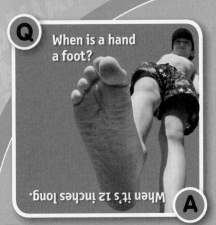

A When it's 12 inches long.

TONGUE TWISTER!

Say this fast three times:

She shares Sheila's cells.

Q Where does a skeleton go for spare parts?

A A secondhand store.

Q How do you wear out your nose?

A Let it run all day.

pun FUN

The **ghost** was **suspicious,** but he couldn't put a **finger** on **why.**

OMAR: When should you definitely get a mole on your back checked out?
SANDY: I don't know, when?
OMAR: When it starts biting you!

LAUGHABLE LIST

IF FRANKENSTEIN'S LAB HAD BEEN AT THE ZOO, HE COULD'VE USED:

☐ Eagle eyes
☐ Crocodile tears
☐ The cat's meow
☐ The bee's knees
☐ Bear feet

Like its relative, the camel, an alpaca walks on two padded toes instead of hooves.

ZARA: I went to give blood yesterday.
RICKY: How did it go?
ZARA: It was all in vein.

Q What does the tooth fairy pay the most money for?

A Buck teeth.

107

Q What did the left foot say to the right foot after scoring a goal in soccer?

A "Toe-nailed it!"

Contortionists know how to get a leg up.

DROOL RULES!

Q What instrument did the skeleton play in the local marching band?

A The trom-bone.

Q Why did the **beekeeper** go to the doctor?

A Because he had hives.

PATIENT: Every time I take a nap, my skin gets red and itchy.
DOCTOR: You need to stop napping in poison ivy.
PATIENT: Don't you think that's a rash decision?

 Q
How do dentists get so smart?

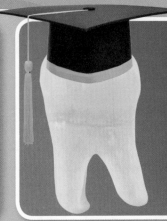

Did you know that human beings produce **two to four pints** (1–2 L) of **saliva** each day?

Saliva helps to keep bad breath at bay.

TONGUE TWISTER!
Say this fast three times:

Fickle Freddie's freckles fit his face.

COACH: Marissa, why are you nodding so much?
MARISSA: You told us to do 15 chin-ups!

PATIENT: Doctor, I feel light-headed, my vision is foggy, and I've developed a fear of planes.
DOCTOR: You need to get your head out of the clouds!

SAY WHAT?

NAME Whiplash

FAVORITE ACTIVITY
Sharpening my teeth

FAVORITE TOY
My tail—it's great
for chasing

PET PEEVE
Losing my grip,
despite having
sharp claws

IS AN
EYE-LESS
IGUANA
CALLED
A GUANA?

IGUANA BE
ORANGE.

WHEN IT
COMES TO
HUMOR, THESE
JOKES ARE OFF
THE SCALES!

An iguana can detach
its tail if caught by
a predator and will
grow another without
permanent damage.

An owl can turn its head 270 degrees, allowing it to look completely over its shoulder.

KNOCK, KNOCK.

Who's there?

Dee.

Dee who?

Dee smile on your face is brilliant!

Q Why did the skeleton go to the barbecue joint?

A He wanted spare ribs.

Q What happened when the hand was caught stealing?

A It was a-wrist-ed.

Q What happens when a diver gets into trouble?

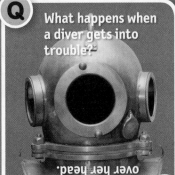

A She finds herself in over her head.

TONGUE TWISTER!

Say this fast three times:

An **itch** which **itches** an **inch**, **itches** which **witch?**

DOCTOR: You've lost 15 pounds. How did you manage that?
PATIENT: I don't know. They just got a weigh from me.

Q What did the pirate say when he finally spotted land?

A "Thar be a sight for shore eyes!"

Q Why was the girl hitting the piano keys with her head?

A She was playing it by ear.

LAUGHABLE LIST

THINGS YOU DON'T WANT TO OVERHEAR DURING SURGERY:

☐ Uh-oh, I'm always mixing up my left and right.

☐ Whoa, should it be doing that?

☐ This doesn't look good at all!

☐ Yuck, blood! It's so gross, and now it's everywhere!

☐ Oops!

Q Why is the **appendix** upset?

A Because it's always put last.

Q How are eyes like teachers?

A They both have pupils.

POLICE: Ma'am, your feet are under arrest.
WOMAN: What for?
POLICE: I heard you say they're killing you.

210   210
200   200
190   190
180   180
170   170
160   160

LAUGHABLE LIST

FOUR REASONS TO GO BAREFOOT:

☐ To give those corns and bunions a break.

☐ Your feet sweat less.

☐ You're always ready for a toe-wrestling match.

☐ Well, who do you know that wears shoes in the shower?

Q What time of day are dentists always booked?

A Tooth-hurty.

Q What did the thigh say to the shin?

A "If you knee-d something, I have a connection."

A hyena's front legs are longer than its back legs, making the animal look as if it is walking uphill.

DINA: Did you hear about the girl whose butt fell off?
LUKE: No, what happened?
DINA: She was really bummed out.

Q Where does the stork deliver baby boys?

A To male boxes.

Q When do feet start tapping to a beat?

A When they hear sole music.

115

LOL
HUMAN BODY

The **BRAIN** can detect the difference between **REAL** LAUGHTER and **FAKE** laughter.

When a **JOKE** is REALLY FUNNY, it may be described as a **sidesplitter**, KNEE-SLAPPER, or **GUT-BUSTER.**

Laughing at a joke requires activity in **FIVE DIFFERENT** areas of the brain.

HA-HA! THAT TICKLES!

THE FUNNY BONE IS ACTUALLY A NERVE THAT RUNS UNDER THE HUMERUS BONE IN THE ARM.

CHAPTER 5

Sidesplitting Science

Scientists in Sweden have launched a study to see if a cat's meows actually mean anything. They are recording the sounds cats make when hungry, content, annoyed, and more to see if any patterns emerge.

NURI: How did you know your computer had a rodent problem?
XAVIER: I followed a trail of crumbs to the mouse pad.

It's **hard** to believe that **atoms** make up **everything**.

STOP, THAT TICKLES!

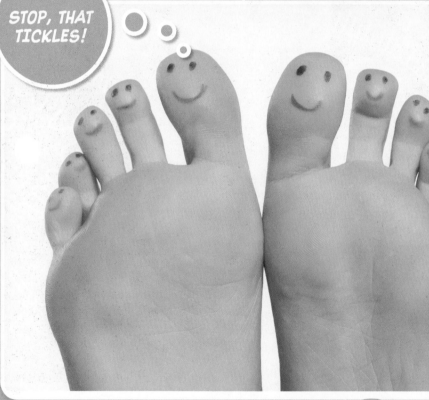

Say this fast three times:

Forrest forces foamy formulas to form.

Q

What do you get when you cross a musician with a chemist?

Someone who works with test tubas.

 A

Q

What kind of dog did the mad scientist create?

A

An Alaskan mala-mutant.

Q

What did the sidewalk say to the earthquake?

HAHA! HAHA! HAHA! HAHA! HAHA! HAHA!

A

"You crack me up!"

Did you know that people's most **ticklish** spots are on the **sides** and **soles of their feet?**

Your foot also has more than a hundred muscles, ligaments, and tendons.

TONGUE TWISTER!

Say this fast three times:

Sue sure sews swell sutures.

sodium

11

Na

22.990

potassium

SAM: Did you memorize any part of the periodic table? SHAWN: Na.

RASHIDA: It's fun to tell stories to scientists.
VALERIE: Why do you say that?
RASHIDA: Because they always have interesting reactions.

121

Q Why didn't the two bears get along in the Arctic?

A They were polar opposites.

Frizzy physicists finish physical feats.

Q When is a chemist like a spy?

A When he's working with a bond.

Q Why did Marie and Pierre become scientists?

A They were naturally Curie-ous.

Q Why did the primatologist quit her job?

A She was tired of the monkey business.

pun FUN

Gas, solid, liquid, plasma, it's a matter of how you look at it.

MABEL: Why did the mad scientist give herself electric shocks?
BLAIR: Ouch! Why?
MABEL: So she could keep up with current events.

Queasy Kesey quit his chemical quiz.

JASMINE: How do you know which home in the neighborhood belongs to a botanist?
DAHLIA: I don't know, how?
JASMINE: It's the green house.

Doctors have used an extract from peacock feathers to treat snakebites.

KNOCK, KNOCK.

Who's there?
Tech.
Tech who?
Tech out my new lab coat!

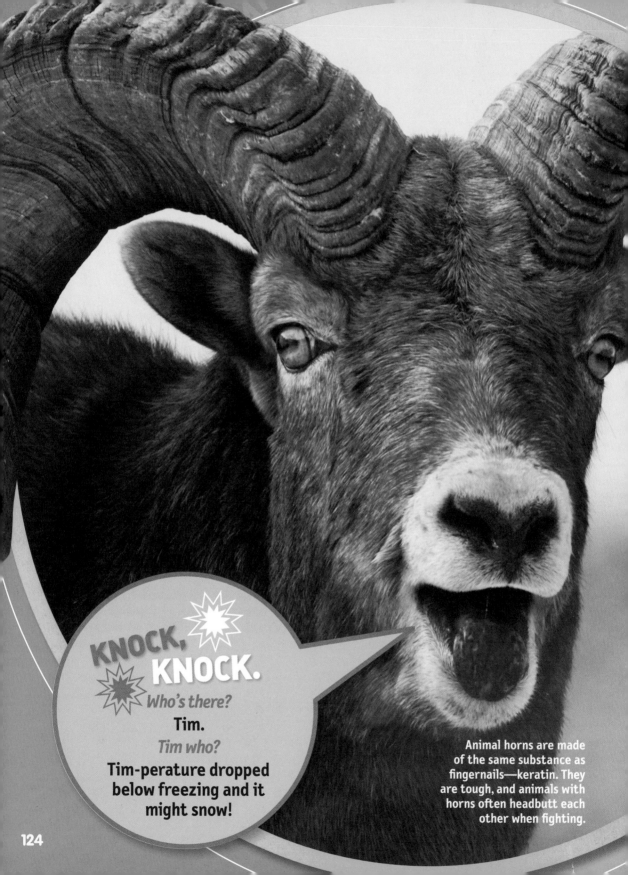

KNOCK, KNOCK.

Who's there?

Tim.

Tim who?

Tim-perature dropped below freezing and it might snow!

Animal horns are made of the same substance as fingernails—keratin. They are tough, and animals with horns often headbutt each other when fighting.

Q Why are robots so fake to one another?

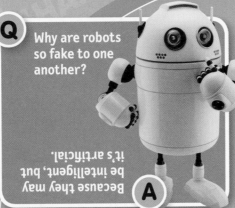

A Because they may be intelligent, but it's artificial.

Q What game do meteorologists like to play?

A Twister.

Q How does a hurricane watch the weather report?

A With its eye.

Q What kind of snack do computers carry?

A Cookies.

GENETICIST: I've identified the most important genetic trait in children.
LAB ASSISTANT: Really?
GENETICIST: Yes, it's the recess trait.

EARTHQUAKE: I'm feeling really shaken up right now.
TECTONIC PLATES: You could say that's our fault.

JAKE: When did the professor become a mad scientist?
TERESA: After his students broke all of his experiments.

LAUGHABLE LIST

SIR ISAAC NEWTON'S THREE
LESSER KNOWN LAWS OF MOTION:

☐ A donut in motion to my mouth will stay in motion until in my stomach.

☐ You cannot force the teacher to budge on a test. The grade carries too much weight.

☐ The teacher's reaction to you chewing gum in class will lead to a Principal's action.

Q Why are felines often the reason for scientific breakthroughs?

A Because they're cat-alysts.

NAME Beakers

FAVORITE ACTIVITY
Experimenting in
the laboratory

FAVORITE TOY
My x-ray glasses

PET PEEVE
Getting too close to
the Bunsen burner

BELIEVE ME, NO-BUNNY REALLY UNDERSTANDS QUANTUM PHYSICS!

OK, REMIND ME, ARE ELECTRONS PAWS-ITIVE OR NEGATIVE?

NEW DISCOVERIES ALWAYS MAKE ME HOPPY!

An average rabbit has 768 smelling genes. That's almost twice as many as a human, which has 392.

Which scientist smelled the best in the mornings?

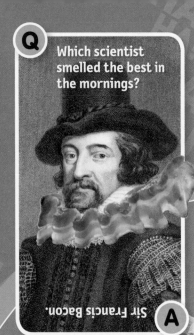

A

Sir Francis Bacon.

pun FUN

Mathematicians have all the problems, but **chemists** have all the **solutions.**

LIZ: Why do doctors go into the field of medicine?
GRACE: I don't know. Tell me, why?
LIZ: Because they want to call the shots.

YIKES, WHICH ONE'S DOLLY?

Q

Why did the
sprinter train
on his computer?

A   It was a laptop with a track pad.

Q What did the pencil say to the sharpener?

A "Get to the point!"

Q How did the **computer fall out** of the building?

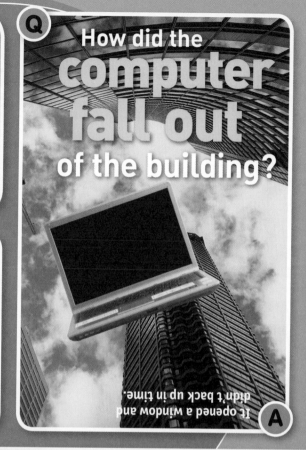

A It opened a window and didn't back up in time.

Did you know that scientists once **cloned** a sheep? Her name was **Dolly.**

People have even cloned champion racehorses!

TONGUE TWISTER!

Say this fast three times:

Vik views a rare whale well.

SUNG: I read that Alexander Graham Bell's first telephone was discovered buried in a graveyard.
ISLA: How did they know it was his?
SUNG: It was a dead ringer.

IT'S FOR YOU!

IT WAS THE LAST FIVE MINUTES OF SCIENCE CLASS, and Mrs. Baines, the teacher, stood up and addressed the students.

"Now, class," Mrs. Baines said. "It's time to turn in your homework on your favorite element."

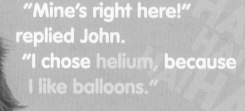

"Mine's right here!" replied John. "I chose helium, because I like balloons."

"Nice work, John," said Mrs. Baines.

"I've got mine, too!" Kate exclaimed. "I chose copper, because that's the name of my dog."

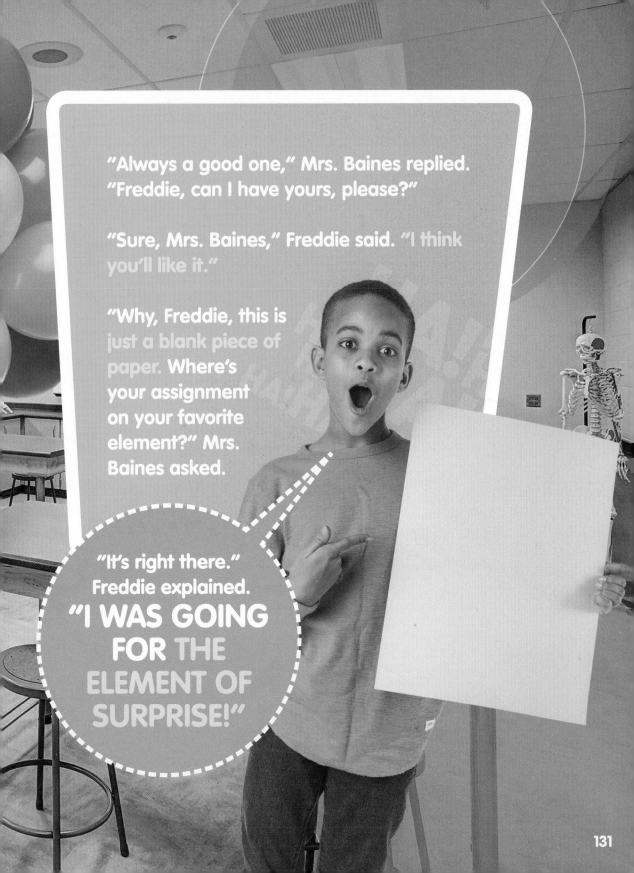

"Always a good one," Mrs. Baines replied. "Freddie, can I have yours, please?"

"Sure, Mrs. Baines," Freddie said. "I think you'll like it."

"Why, Freddie, this is just a blank piece of paper. Where's your assignment on your favorite element?" Mrs. Baines asked.

"It's right there." Freddie explained. "I WAS GOING FOR THE ELEMENT OF SURPRISE!"

KNOCK, KNOCK.

Who's there?
Mack.
Mack who?
Mack the science jokes
stop already!

Some species of wrasse grow
to be seven feet (2 m) long. That's
equal to the height of a door.

Q How do scientists keep their dogs in the yard without a leash?

A They use a force field.

pun FUN

Microbiologists are very cultured.

VICKI: How do scientists celebrate their birthdays?
DOUG: How?
VICKI: With party-cles.

Q What happened when the volcano got the flu?

A He spewed.

Q What kind of cats do computers like best?

A Tab-keys.

Q Where does the science club eat in the cafeteria?

A At the periodic table.

Q Why did the thermometer go to college?

A To get a higher degree.

LAUGHABLE LIST

SCIENCE BOOKS WE WANT TO READ:

- ☐ *Rock Stars: The Underground Tour* by Jim Ologist
- ☐ *Turbo Tornados* by Gale Force and Wendy Day
- ☐ *Dissecting the School Lunch* by Pete Treedisch
- ☐ *How Small Does It All* by Molly Culer

135

Q How do scientists measure the intelligence of bonobos?

A They give them ape-titude tests.

Q Why was the scientist's assistant covered in fur?

A The assistant was a Lab-rador.

Q How did the meteorologist sew his new raincoat?

A Using a weather pattern.

Q How did the engineer win the boat race?

A She used row-bots.

Q What did the biologist give her friend who had bad breath?

A Experi-mints.

Geologists don't just take their jobs for granite.

Biologists have good cell service.

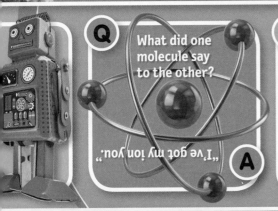

Q What did one molecule say to the other?

A "I've got my ion you."

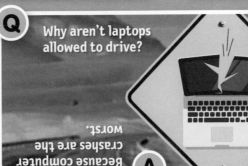

Q Why aren't laptops allowed to drive?

A Because computer crashes are the worst.

NOW THAT'S AN ILLUMINATING THOUGHT!

Did you know that your **brain** generates enough electricity to power a **lightbulb**?

Countless electrical signals zap between our brain cells.

LAUGHABLE LIST

PHILOSOPHY OF A CHEMISTRY TEACHER:

- ☐ Here today, argon tomorrow.
- ☐ In for a nickel, in for a dime.
- ☐ Life goes on ... xenon, and on, and on.
- ☐ Grin and barium it.
- ☐ I zinc, therefore I am.
- ☐ Don't skate on tin ice.

SAY WHAT?

NAME **Snapper**

FAVORITE ACTIVITY
Ornithology—that's bird-watching to you!

FAVORITE TOY
A pair of binoculars

PET PEEVE
Migrating season

A CROCODILE WALKED INTO A CHEMISTRY LAB, BUT THERE WAS NO REACTION.

CROCODILES WORK HARDER THAN COMPUTERS BECAUSE THEY HAVE MORE BYTES.

EVERY LABORATORY NEEDS A CROCODILE CLIP OR TWO!

KNOCK, KNOCK.

Who's there?
Unit.
Unit who?
Unit-ting a sweater?
I'd love one, too!

Scientists have learned that crocodiles pile sticks on their snouts to lure nest-building birds. The reptiles snap up the birds as they approach to take a stick.

IS A CROCODILE WITH GPS A NAVI-GATOR?

139

Q What kind of glowing insect do you find in a science lab?

A A radi-ant.

Q What did the little magnet say to the big magnet?

A "Wow, the force is strong with you!"

Q Why did the student fall asleep during the computer class?

A Because it was cy-boring.

pun FUN

Our teacher linked the **zoology lessons** together using an **animal food chain.**

LITTLE SISTER: Ugh, why is Tom better at floating than I am?
MOTHER: Because your big brother has more boy-ancy.

BETHANY: There's a species that connects humans to cats.
KAY: Really?
BETHANY: Yes, it's called the missing lynx.

TONGUE TWISTER!

Say this fast three times:

Hugh knew dissection like the shoe section.

Q What did the scientist study to create artificially intelligent plants?

A Ro-botany.

140

KNOCK, KNOCK.

Who's there?
Air.
Air who?
Air I am, where are you?

The brown bear's scientific name is *Ursus arctos*. *Ursus* means "bear" in Latin and *arctos* comes from the Greek word for bear.

KNOCK, KNOCK.

Who's there?

Watt.

Watt who?

Watt will you do when we run out of science jokes?

It is thanks to strong, muscular hindquarters that a Jack Russell can jump up to five times its own height.

KARL: Did you hear about the piece of carbon that turned into a diamond?

OWEN: No, what happened?

KARL: It couldn't handle the pressure.

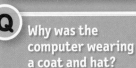

Q Why was the computer wearing a coat and hat?

A It was code inside.

Q Where did the scientist find the solution to his problem?

A In the back pocket of his genes.

TONGUE TWISTER!

Say this fast three times:

A measure is missing, Miss.

Q Why are neutrons wealthy?

A Because they never get charged.

Q What do you call a sibling who is always coming up with ideas?

A A hypothe-sister.

Q What do you get when you cross a computer and a sheep?

A A lot of RAM.

LAUGHABLE LIST

QUESTIONS SCIENTISTS STILL HAVEN'T SOLVED:

☐ What does go bump in the night?

☐ Who has the world's smelliest armpit?

☐ Are we there yet?

☐ I know you are, but what am I? No, really, what am I?

☐ Is the person who smelt it really the one who dealt it?

143

LOL SCIENCE

SCIENTISTS HAVE discovered that RATS LAUGH WHEN THEY'RE **TICKLED.**

GELOTOLOGY IS THE STUDY OF **LAUGHTER.**

BRAIN SCANS show that laughter IS **CONTAGIOUS.**

OXFORD DICTIONARIES SELECTED AN **EMOJI** OF A FACE WITH **TEARS OF JOY** AS THE **WORD** OF THE YEAR IN **2015.**

KOKO THE **GORILLA** understands English and SIGN LANGUAGE so WELL THAT SHE CAN MAKE **JOKES.**

CHAPTER 6

Nutty Nature

HA!HA!HA!HA!HA!
HA!HA!HA!HA!
HA!HA!HA!
HA!HA!

Q What did the boulder name its son?

A Rocky.

Q What did the clouds put on after their rain shower?

A Thunderwear.

KAMMI: Why did a bunch of felines gather on Broadway?
STEVEN: I have no idea, tell me.
KAMMI: Because they love mew-sicals!

TONGUE TWISTER!

Say this fast three times:

Moses hoses his rows of roses.

TOMMY: Where would you find a blue-ringed octopus?
MOM: In the ocean.
TOMMY: Can you be more Pacific?

Did you know that **humming-birds** can flap their wings **up to 80 times** a second?

The heart of some humming-birds can beat more than 1,000 times a minute.

Q How do killer whales hunt their prey?

A In a very orca-strated manner.

PLATYPUS: I'll take two pairs of boots, a hat, and a pair of sunglasses.
SHOPKEEPER: Great. How would you like to pay?
PLATYPUS: Just put it on my bill.

GIVE IT A REST, ALREADY!

NEAL: Why did the forest ranger carry a hairbrush on the job?
FRANKIE: Because he was always fixing his hair?
NEAL: No, to work on the fur trees.

Q Why do flowers smell so fresh?

A Because they're potty-trained.

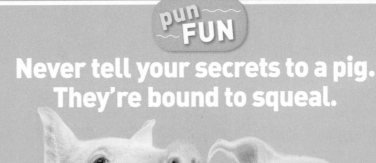

pun FUN

Never tell your secrets to a pig. They're bound to squeal.

149

TONGUE TWISTER!

Say this fast three times:

Minuscule mussels must muster muscles.

Q Why are marine animals successful in business?

A They know how to seal the deal.

SANJAY: Did you hear about the bats that found humans digging in their cave?
TYLER: No, were the bats able to get rid of the people?
SANJAY: Yes, it was a miner problem.

VALERIE: Did you see the pod of humpback whales jumping out of the water?
SHAM: Shucks, I missed them.
VALERIE: Too bad. They showed all the tell-tail signs.

Q Why do kangaroos take yoga classes?

A To calm their jumpy nerves.

Q What's a camel's favorite nursery rhyme?

A Humpty Dumpty.

Q What do snakes call their prey?

A Ssssscrumptioussss.

Q What does a bird of prey say when it bumps into something in the dark?

A "Ow-l!"

pun FUN

The ocean is so friendly. It always waves.

Polar bears are the largest living meat-eaters on Earth.

KNOCK, KNOCK.

Who's there?
Floe.
Floe who?
No, there's an ice floe ahead. We better turn soon!

A newborn kangaroo is called a joey and is about the size of a cherry at birth.

KNOCK, KNOCK.

Who's there?
Kanga.
Kanga who?
No, it's Kangaroo.

Q What do you call a snowman on summer vacation?

A A puddle.

TONGUE TWISTER!

Say this fast three times:

Sharp shirts, sharper sharks.

MYA: Why aren't pigs allowed to play sports?
AVERY: Because they can't drive to the games?
MYA: No, because they hog the ball.

KYNDEL: Rabbits can win any kind of race.
CHASE: No way.
KYNDEL: Yeah, lots of close races are won by a hare.

Q What did one cat say to the other cat after dinner?

A "You have a little mouse-tache left on your lip."

Q What did the bull say to his friend when she got too excited?

A "Don't have a cow!"

Q What does a **wildebeest** say when it gets an answer **right**?

A "I gnu it!"

Q How do you know when a hive is in a hurry?

A They're making a beeline for their destination.

LAUGHABLE LIST

CHEETAH'S LIST OF COMPLAINTS:

☐ Elephant snores too loudly.

☐ Vulture never washes his feet.

☐ There are always bugs on my food.

☐ No one believes me when I win fair and square.

153

NAME Smiler

FAVORITE ACTIVITY
Shedding my skin
once a month

FAVORITE TOY
Anything I can
climb up

PET PEEVE
Not being able to
change color

GECK-OVER YOURSELF!

CALL ME COLD-BLOODED, BUT I COULD SNAP UP A SPIDER RIGHT NOW.

Most geckos don't
have eyelids and use
their tongues to
clean their eyes.

154

155

JAMES: Do you know what's bigger than three hippos and can only be spotted at night with a flashlight?
KATE: No, what?
JAMES: Their shadows.

pun FUN

The tree felt sappy listening to the love song.

I'M ALL HEART!

Q Why did the birds laugh at the dog?

He was barking up the wrong tree. **A**

JULIE: Why aren't pigs allowed to stay out late?
SOL: Okay, I have no idea.
JULIE: Because they have really strict parents.

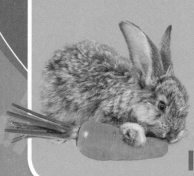

pun FUN

The rabbit gave his love a 24-carrot ring. It was delicious.

Q What do you call two boa constrictors that have a crush on each other?

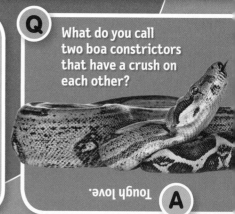

Tough love. **A**

Did you know that a **giraffe's** heart is **two feet** (0.6 m) long and weighs **25 pounds** (11 kg)?

That's not the only giant thing about giraffes: Their hooves are the size of dinner plates!

Q Why did the bee take driving lessons?

A To become a buzz driver.

TONGUE TWISTER!

Say this fast three times:

Seth's short shark shrank.

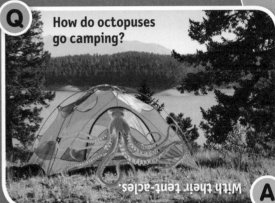

Q How do octopuses go camping?

A With their tent-acles.

Q What do canaries say on Halloween?

A "Trick or tweet!"

Q What did one mushroom say to the other at the movies?

A "Are you lichen this as much as I am?"

157

ONE AFTERNOON, A FARMER WAS MILKING HIS COWS. While working on the last cow, Bessie, he accidentally squirted himself in the eye.

He jerked his head up, bumping into Bessie. Startled, she ran off, knocking the milk pail over, bursting through the barn doors, and sprinting out into the pasture.

The other cows watched. Then they too raced out of the barn, knocking over their milk pails and the farmer.

The farmer staggered to his feet, surveying the spilled milk and hay scattered all over the floor.

Then he peered out the barn doors to see his cows disappearing over the horizon. Shaking his head, he muttered a few words:

"What an udder failure."

Q What game do rabbits play at recess?

A Hopscotch.

Q What do you call a yeti that's been working out all winter?

A Abdominal Snowman.

Q How do flowers kiss?

A With their tulips.

Q How do you **know whether** a **duck thinks** you're **funny?**

A It quacks up when you tell a joke.

Q How do you know there's an elephant in your house?

A There's a giant hole in the wall.

ALINA: A new Tex-Mex restaurant opened in Antarctica.
DERRICK: Cool, what does it have?
ALINA: *Brrritos.*

Q What happened when the two beaches played each other?

A They tide.

STAN: Why aren't pigs allowed to drive?
LUKE: Because they can't reach the pedals?
STAN: No, because they hog the road.

Incredibly strong, the Samoyed dog from Siberia was originally bred to pull sleds.

KNOCK, KNOCK.

Who's there?

Alpaca.

Alpaca who?

Alpaca sandwich for you if you join me on a picnic.

KNOCK, KNOCK.

Who's there?

Goose.

Goose who?

I don't need to guess. I already know who you are.

Geese fly high in V formations. When on the ground, a group of geese is called a gaggle.

Q Why did all the children run outside with leashes?

A The weatherman said it was raining cats and dogs.

TONGUE TWISTER!
Say this fast three times:

Phil feels he heals eels.

Q How did the explorer lose his car in the jungle?

A It was eaten by a car-nivorous plant.

BAT: Owl is so nosy.
OPOSSUM: Why do you think that?
BAT: Because every time I tell him something, he asks, "Who, who?"

Q How can you tell when a penguin is happy?

A It has a big pen-grin.

WALRUS #1: Wait a minute. Something smells fishy.
WALRUS #2: We better investigate. I'm hungry!

Q Why can't Earth take big tests?

A Because it cracks under pressure.

LAUGHABLE LIST

BAD GIFTS TO GIVE A SNAKE ON ITS BIRTHDAY:

☐ Basketball
☐ Scissors
☐ Pants
☐ Jump rope
☐ Pet mongoose

Q Where do all the cool woodpeckers meet up?

A At the poplar tree.

Q Why did the **elephant** join a **band?**

A Because it trumpeted.

 pun **FUN**

Hedgehogs know how to spike a ball.

TONGUE TWISTER!

Say this fast three times:

Sheep sleep seven a side.

YOU'RE HISSS-TORY!

AMBER: What happens when a snake doesn't get what it wants?
IRFAN: What?
AMBER: It has a hissy fit.

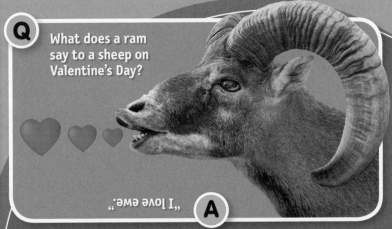

Q What does a ram say to a sheep on Valentine's Day?

A "I love ewe."

Q What did the giraffe say when another giraffe started munching on its tree?

A "Scram, this is my neck of the woods!"

MMM, SO TASTY!

Did you know that a **hippo** can open its mouth wide enough for a four-foot (1.2-m)-tall **kid** to fit inside?

A hippo's lips are about two feet (0.6 m) wide!

JULIA: Do you know how rabbits can fly?
BRIAN: How?
JULIA: They take hare-planes.

Q What did the **dogs love** about **performing onstage?**

A A-paws from the audience.

NAME Acorn and Hazel

FAVORITE ACTIVITY Burying nuts for winter food

FAVORITE TOY A spade for digging

PET PEEVE Rocky ground

I LOVE TO SQUIRREL AWAY FOOD.

I COULD GO NUTS FOR A SNACK RIGHT NOW!

I'M JUST STOPPING HERE WHILE I PAWS TO ADMIRE THE VIEW.

YOU'LL HAVE TO EXCUSE ME, I DON'T ALWAYS TALK WITH MY MOUTH FULL!

KNOCK, KNOCK.

Who's there?

May.

May who?

May I please come in now?

Squirrels have cheek pouches for collecting food to store in their underground burrows.

Q Which **dinosaurs** were **singers** and **poets**?

A Rap-tors.

Q Why aren't elephants allowed at public pools?

A Because they wear their trunks on their heads.

Q What do you call a polar bear in the desert?

A Lost.

Q Where do tortoises shop?

A At hard-wear stores.

Q How can you tell when there's a hyena in your house?

A You hear her laughing at your school photo.

Q How did the animals escape from the zoo?

A They used mon-keys.

Q What did the tornado say to the clouds?

A "Want to go for a spin?"

JACKSON: Did you know the king of the jungle's first job was as a news reporter?
HENRY: Really? Was he any good?
JACKSON: No, no one believed any of his stories because he was always lion.

Q How do sloths stay healthy?

A They don't eat fast food.

168

Ducklings grow adult feathers at around two months old.

KNOCK,
KNOCK.
Who's there?
Beehive.
Beehive who?
**Beehive yourself
and open the door.**

Grizzly bears can run
up to 30 miles an hour
(48 km/h). That's faster
than a horse.

Q

How do you **raise** a **hippo?**

A With a sturdy crane.

Q

Where do emperor penguins go swimming?

A The South Pool.

Q Why aren't horses allowed to vote?

A They're neigh-sayers.

Q **Where** did **the bird** catch a **cold?**

A On a sick-amore tree.

Q What do you call a reptile that can't walk straight?

A A crookedile.

Q Why didn't the sea anemone ever go anywhere?

A It didn't have the guts.

LEAH: What happened when the cow grounded its calf for a week?
ROHINI: What?
LEAH: The calf was *moody* the entire time.

TONGUE TWISTER!

Say this fast three times:

Frilled lizards lounge lazily.

LOL NATURE

I'M HAVING A BALL!

A CROCODILE can't stick its **TONGUE OUT** at you.

JAPANESE MACAQUES make snowballs **FOR FUN.**

SPOTTED HYENAS make a noise that sounds like a **HUMAN LAUGH** when they are **NERVOUS** or **EXCITED.**

ELEPHANTS have a sense of **HUMOR.**

THE **HAPPY-FACE** SPIDER, *THERIDION GRALLATOR*, GOT ITS NAME FROM THE **SMILEY DESIGN ON ITS ABDOMEN.**

CHAPTER 7

Amusing Athletics

HA!HA!HA!HA!
HA!HA!HA!HA!HA!
HA!HA!HA!
HA!HA!HA!

KNOCK, KNOCK.

Who's there?

Ali.

Ali who?

Ali-oop—that's the maneuver for me.

An elephant shows that it wants to play by crouching down and wiggling its head from side to side. There is even an elephant in Thailand who likes to shoot hoops. Her name is Nung Ning.

Q Which sport do spiders like best?

A Cricket.

I'd run away from school, but then my **gym teacher** would know I've been **faking** being lousy at sports.

BRI: Did you see what happened to the last crew team during the regatta?
ALLYSON: No, what?
BRI: Half the rowers lost their paddles.
ALLYSON: Oh, no. What an oar-deal!

Did you know that a **bowling pin** has to tilt by about **10 degrees** to fall down?

Did you know that three back-to-back strikes in bowling is called a turkey?

SMASHED IT!

Q What does the **basketball** team do when it gets **hungry**?

A The coach sends in subs.

Q Where do track-and-field athletes lock up their gold medals?

A In a pole vault.

TONGUE TWISTER!

Say this fast three times:

Kit kicks six kicks quickly.

Q Why do **golfers carry two of everything?**

A Because they might get a hole in one!

pun FUN

Sumo wrestling is an event of grand proportions.

KNOCK, KNOCK.

Who's there?
Linus.
Linus who?
Linus up and get ready to race!

HA!HA!HA!HA!
HA!HA!
HA!HA!

Toucans are skilled climbers, thanks to two backward-pointing toes on each foot.

Q Why are chickens bad at baseball?

A They only hit fowl balls.

SCOTT: Never believe stories told by basketball players.
HEIDI: Why?
SCOTT: Because they're all tall tales.

Q Why was the softball player happy when she got a strike?

A She was bowling!

LAUGHABLE LIST

AUTOBIOGRAPHIES OF ANIMAL COACHES:

- ☐ *Never Say Die* by Kat O'Nine-Lives
- ☐ *Get Your Head Out of the Clouds and Into the Game* by Ger Affe
- ☐ *Crush the Competition* by Elle E. Fant and Ally Gater
- ☐ *Always a Winner* by Ima Cheetah

JOSH: Did you hear what happened when a fan yelled at the pole-vaulter during a meet?
RYAN: No, what?
JOSH: The pole-vaulter flew off the handle.

LISA: Did you hear about the alpine skier who won the gold medal?
ANDREA: No, what happened to her?
LISA: Her career went downhill after that.

MATT: Ice hockey is more polite than people think.
LARRY: How so?
MATT: After a player elbows someone, the ref serves him penal-tea in a box by himself.

Q Why couldn't the fisherman catch the octopus?

A Because it was armed.

KNOCK, KNOCK.

Who's there?

Gwen.

Gwen who?

Gwen does the race start?

Macaques are nimble-fingered animals. Sneaky ones in India have been known to pick pockets.

Q Why was there a yoga class on the racecourse?

A They were in the home stretch.

SALESPERSON: Welcome to the Carpet Emporium! How can I help you?

WIDE RECEIVER: I'm looking for a throw rug.

Q Which animal is best at baseball?

A A bat.

LAUGHABLE LIST

OLYMPIC SPORTS WE WISH WERE REAL:

- ☐ Unicycling
- ☐ Synchronized surfing
- ☐ Yard sale-ing
- ☐ Breakfast table tennis
- ☐ Go-kart racing
- ☐ Equestrian jumping with miniature horses

Q What do you call a dinosaur that doesn't finish a marathon?

A Tricera-stops.

TONGUE TWISTER!

Say this fast three times:

Pop fly to wide right side.

SON: I just don't understand sports.

MOM: What are you saying?

SON: You use your hands for handball and your feet for football, but which body part is a volley or a basket?

Q What game do birds like to play?

A Air hawk-ey.

Q What did the woman yell to the kids playing tennis in her front yard?

A "Stop all that racket!"

SAY WHAT?

NAME **Little Tweeters**

FAVORITE ACTIVITY
Cheerleading

FAVORITE TOY
Our pom-poms

PET PEEVE
When the whistle blows for the game to start

MY FAVORITE SOCCER POSITION IS THE WINGBACK.

RUNNING TOO FAST CAN GET A BIRDY A-HUFFIN' AND A-PUFFIN.

Swallows nest in rock crevices, tree cavities, and caves.

Q Why wasn't the

soccer player

upset when she missed the penalty shot?

A Because she got a kick out of it.

Q Why was the fullback always on time?

A Because he was always rushing.

FARAH: What do you call a waterskiing crocodile?
MARSHALL: I don't know, what?
FARAH: I don't know either, but if you see one you better get out of the way!

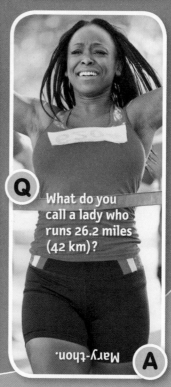

Q What do you call a lady who runs 26.2 miles (42 km)?

A Mary-thon.

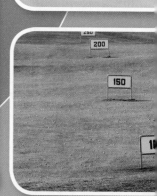

250
200
150
1

Bowlers know how to get the ball **rolling.**

Why do **golfers' clothes** always look so **nice** and **crisp?**

They use nine irons. **A**

Did you know that Surya Bonaly is the only **figure skater** to have landed a **backflip** on just **one skate?**

The highest number of spins made in just one minute is a record-breaking 342.

YES, BUT WHICH FOOT? LEFT OR RIGHT?

TONGUE TWISTER!

Say this fast three times:

Theo throws three free throws.

Q

Where do **golfers learn** how to operate a **car?**

At a driving range. **A**

185

A MAGICIAN TRAVELED TO THE WORLD CUP to watch his favorite team compete in the final match. During the first half, the forward on the rival team scored.

The magician frowned with disappointment and grumbled to himself. Twenty minutes later, the rival forward scored again.

The magician's face grew red with anger. Now his team was losing by two goals, and the referee blew the whistle to end the half.

During the second half, the magician's team looked like they might score. But suddenly, the rival team's star forward intercepted the ball and scored a hat trick! The magician was stunned. He jumped up and shouted, "Unbelievable!"

In a mad frenzy, the magician took off his hat and started to pull his hare out. It was tricky, but security stepped in to stop the magician. A guard took him to one side, saying:

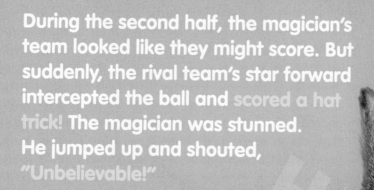

"Forgive me, sir, but you are getting sleight-ly out of hand."

KNOCK, KNOCK.

Who's there?
Tennis.
Tennis who?
Tennis a good time for breakfast, don't you think?

Traditional shuttlecocks for the game of badminton have cones made from real goose feathers. They are still used in professional matches.

Q

Why are golfers always hungry at a pizza party?

A Because they're used to avoiding slices.

ANNA: Do you know what happens when hockey players slip on the ice?
QUINN: No, what?
ANNA: They fall head over heels in gloves.

---

pun FUN

The faster you run, the harder it is to catch your breath.

Q

Why did the **detective** want to question the **softball pitcher?**

A He had seen her underhanded practices.

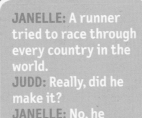

JANELLE: A runner tried to race through every country in the world.
JUDD: Really, did he make it?
JANELLE: No, he couldn't find the Finnish line.

LAUGHABLE LIST

BAD REFEREE CALLS OFF THE FIELD:

☐ Ordering a pizza from a Thai restaurant

☐ Telling a long-winded story without knowing the phone is on mute

☐ Video-chatting while holding the phone to an ear

☐ Pocket-dialing all phone contacts repeatedly

AMIT: What is the hardest part of weightlifting?
LOLA: The training?
AMIT: No, the weights!

---

pun FUN

If you haven't tried **soccer,** you should take a **shot at it.**

Q How is a volleyball player like a waiter?

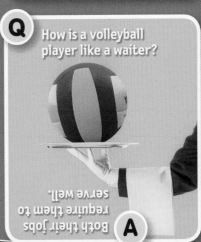

A Both their jobs require them to serve well.

189

Weddell seals are excellent swimmers. They can hold their breath for up to 80 minutes.

KNOCK, KNOCK.

Who's there?
Putter.
Putter who?
Putter there and let's shake on it!

Q Why did the athlete bring a steamroller to the game?

A She wanted to level the playing field.

LAUGHABLE LIST

NOT-SO-FAMOUS SPORTS BOOKS:

- ☐ *Twists, Tumbles, and Terrible Wedgies* by Jim Nasticks
- ☐ *Racing With a Walrus on Your Head* by Barry Strong
- ☐ *Total Misses and Lost Championships* by Anita Du Over

Q Why don't hurricanes compete in sports?

A They would blow the competition away.

Q Why are so many baseball players in jail?

A Because they're paid to steal bases.

Q Why did the student bring scissors to the tryouts?

A She wanted to make the cut.

SONIA: What kind of music did the Olympian play after she won?
FLO: Tell me.
SONIA: Heavy medal.

Q What did the nervous track athlete say before the final race?

A "I think I'm going to hurdle."

Q What do you call a dinosaur that runs a marathon?

A Try-ran-now-sore-us.

191

Q How do sports teams get out of trouble?

A With a very strong defense.

VIVE LE TOUR!

The cyclists are pumped for the Tour de France.

Q Why are magnets good at rock-climbing?

A Because they're naturals at repelling.

CAN ANYONE SEE WHERE WE'RE GOING?

Q Why were there so many **zucchinis** at the tryouts?

A To form a squash team.

192

Q Why did the lady attack the stuffed animals at the carnival?

A She was a prizefighter.

Did you know that there are **two** sports in which teams have to move backward? They are **rowing** and **tug-of-war**.

Tug-of-war was once an Olympic sport!

Q Why did the batter carry a stool with him?

A So he could step up to the plate.

pun FUN

Scuba divers have a depth of knowledge.

Q What's a kangaroo's top track-and-field event?

A The long jump.

193

SAY WHAT?

NAME Titch

FAVORITE ACTIVITY
Fly-fishing

FAVORITE TOY
Fly-fishing rod

PET PEEVE
When the fish gets to
the fly before I do

FANCY A GAME OF LEAPFROG?

FROGS ARE GOOD AT BASKETBALL BECAUSE THEY CAN MAKE ALL THE JUMP SHOTS.

A FROG'S FAVORITE SPORT IS CROAK-ET.

Tree frogs hang upside
down on leaves—like
acrobats—thanks to
sticky disks on their
fingers and toes.

Q

**How did the
golfer prank
her buddy?**

A She gave him a wedgie.

ISIAH: Which cycling jersey
is always a winner?
J.D.: I don't know. How can
you tell something like that?
ISIAH: It's the one with the
name Victor E. on the back.

Q Why don't
basketball players
have passports?

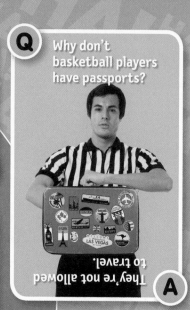

They're not allowed
to travel. **A**

Q

Why did the
baseball manager
recruit a cook for
his team?

He wanted a
good batter. **A**

---

pun
FUN

**Mountain
climbers
have to come
to grips with
where they are.**

Q What did the coach
say to the goalie
during tryouts?

"You're a keeper." **A**

Q Why do bowlers
love Thanksgiving?

It's the one time
of the year they
definitely get a
turkey. **A**

Q What's the name of
the slowest person
in a foot race?

Walker. **A**

IMAN: Why was there a
team of hairdressers at
the Winter Olympics?
COLIN: Why?
IMAN: They were
the curling team
from Brusha.

Cats are natural high jumpers. They can leap up to five times their own height in one bound.

KNOCK, KNOCK.

Who's there?
Jason.
Jason who?
Jason after you is no sweat!

KNOCK, KNOCK.

Who's there?

Iran.

Iran who?

Iran all the way here, but I'm going to need a ride home.

A white-tailed deer can jump a distance of 30 feet (9 m) in a single bound. That's the length of an average school bus.

Q Why did the athlete have to chase down his drink?

A It was running water.

Q What do sailors and baseball players have in common?

A They both stand on deck.

HARRY: You and I should have a little golf tournament.
REX: I'll take you on.
HARRY: Putter there, let's shake on it!

Q Why did the girl wear a tracksuit to her final exam?

A In case she needed to jog her memory.

Q Why was the boy excited about going to the baseball game?

A He heard there might be slides there.

AISHA: What game is a porcupine good at?
EVIE: I don't know.
AISHA: Keep-away.

---

pun FUN

Win or lose, trampolinists will always bounce back.

Q How does a martial arts trainer get to class?

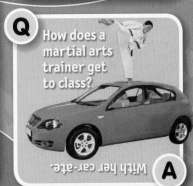

A With her car-ate.

WES: What do you call the game in which your dogs are pulling on the same rope toy?
MAGGIE: Pug-o-war.

LOL SPORTS

IT'S A HOME RUN!

In a **SPORT** called **JOGGLING**, joggers **JUGGLE THREE BALLS AS THEY RUN.**

BASEBALL UMPIRES originally wore **TAILED** coats and **TOP HATS.**

At an annual **REGATTA** in Canada, **BOATERS RACE** each other in giant **PUMPKINS.**

In a **GURNING** competition, participants **TRY TO WIN** by making the **UGLIEST FACE POSSIBLE.**

IN **2015,** A HERD OF CATTLE SAUNTERED ONTO THE PATH OF CYCLISTS COMPETING IN THE **TOUR DE FRANCE.**

HEY! MOOOOVE OVER.

CHAPTER 8

Gross Gags

Q What does everyone wear at a toilet's birthday?

A Potty hats.

pun FUN

Gastropods move slowly when they feel sluggish.

Q How do skunks say goodbye to each other?

A "Smell ya later!"

OOPS, I FORGOT MY DEODORANT TODAY!

Q How do you wish a **centipede** good luck?

A "Break a leg, leg, leg, leg, leg, leg ...!"

Q What does the booger say to the nose?

A "You blow me away!"

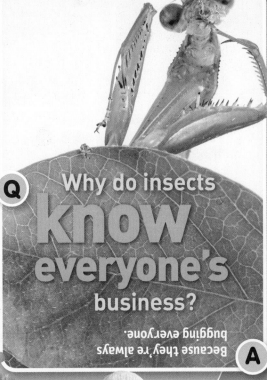

Q Why do insects **know** everyone's business?

A Because they're always bugging everyone.

Did you know that **turkey vultures** throw up on purpose to defend themselves? The **vomit** grosses out their enemies and keeps them away.

These amazing birds have a wingspan of six feet (2 m)!

Q Why did the frog eat the firefly?

A It wanted a light snack.

Q Where do you take a ghost for vacation?

A The Dead Sea.

TONGUE TWISTER!

Say this fast three times:

Who offers awful alfalfa?

Q Where do you take a zombie for vacation?

A The Undead Sea.

TONGUE TWISTER!

Say this fast three times:

Five fat flies fled three fleas.

Q What do you call a monster that smells weird and snores really loudly in its sleep?

A Dad.

Q What was the insect's review of the roach motel?

A He gave it a rot-ten rating.

Q What did the gravedigger give his wife for Valentine's Day?

A Corpse flowers.

Q Why can't you hear a pterodactyl going to the bathroom?

A Because it has a silent p.

Q What does a sailor say when he sees a trash barge?

A "Land filly!"

FELIX: Originally, the story of Cinderella was about a cat.
ELLA: No, really?
FELIX: Yes, and she was running away from a hairball.

PRIYANKA: What do bloodsucking creatures recite in school?
OTTO: I don't know. Tell me, what?
PRIYANKA: The pledge of a-leech-ance.

TONGUE TWISTER!

Say this fast three times:

Betty bit a black bug, but it bit her back.

LAUGHABLE LIST

THINGS YOU DEFINITELY SHOULDN'T WEAR AS A HAT:

☐ A pizza
☐ A spiderweb
☐ A blobfish
☐ A used diaper
☐ Porcupines

Spiny katydids are covered in sharp spikes, which they use to jab at their enemies.

KNOCK, KNOCK.

Who's there?

Snot.

Snot who?

Snot nice to make someone wait.

People used to believe that you could relieve a toothache by kissing a donkey.

TONGUE TWISTER!

Say this
fast three times:

A swarm swam ashore.

CHUCK: Coach, I'm feeling too sick to climb the rope today.
COACH: Up, Chuck!

 Q What did the monster make for dessert?

Coconut slime pie. **A**

Q Why did the spiders team up together?

Because they saw eye to eye to eye to eye to eye to eye to eye to eye to eye to eye to eye to eye to eye to eye. **A**

pun FUN

Sewage is a waste of resources.

JOANNA: I heard Frankenstein planned to go to college so that he could be smarter.
LILY: Did he graduate?
JOANNA: No, he changed his mind.

DOG #1: Why are you covered in drool?
DOG #2: I was standing in front of the spitz.

DINER: Waitress, there's a hare on my plate!
WAITRESS: Yes, sir, you ordered the rabbit.

I'M NOT KOALA-FIED TO BE WRITING JOKES!

I'M SO ITCHY, THIS TREE MUST BE INFESTED WITH AN ANT KOALANY.

KNOCK, KNOCK.

Who's there?
Dan.
Dan who?
Dan-druff is all over your head and shoulders.

A baby koala's first solid food is pap—a mush of decomposed eucalyptus leaves produced by its mother.

211

Q

What did the mad
biologist
use to wrap
presents?

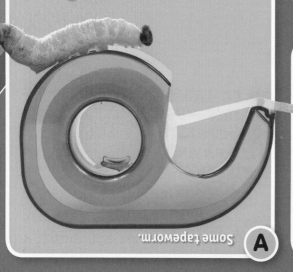

Some tapeworm. **A**

Q

What kind of jewelry do enemies give each other?

Ringworms. **A**

TONGUE TWISTER!

Say this fast three times:

Sixty-six
sticky
skeletons.

Did you know that head lice **suck blood** from your scalp? That's what causes the intense **itching.**

A head louse is about the same size as a sesame seed.

LAUGHABLE LIST

FIVE ANSWERS TO THE QUESTION "WHAT STINKS?":

- ☐ Your brother's gym sneakers
- ☐ Your mom's new mystery casserole
- ☐ That tuna sandwich you've had at the bottom of your backpack ... all month
- ☐ The "puppy" your friend saved that turned out to be a skunk
- ☐ Homework on a snow day

DYLAN: I might be deathly afraid of spiders.
CRYSTAL: Have you checked the symptoms for arachnophobia?
DYLAN: I was going to look them up on the Internet, until I heard it was full of websites.

They may be small,
but arachnids have
a lot of mite.

What did the big
green monster
say after she
embarrassed
herself in front of
the whole school?

"My life is
totally ogre!" **A**

MMM,
LUNCH!

TONGUE
TWISTER!

Say this
fast three times:

Six slick slimy snots.

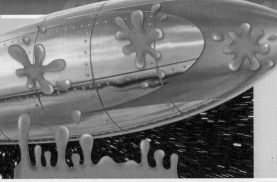

Q

How do you
send a **booger**
to space?

On a snot rocket. **A**

213

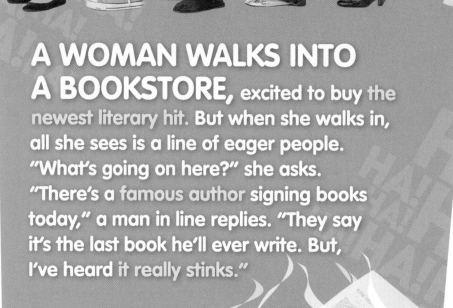

A WOMAN WALKS INTO A BOOKSTORE, excited to buy the newest literary hit. But when she walks in, all she sees is a line of eager people. "What's going on here?" she asks. "There's a famous author signing books today," a man in line replies. "They say it's the last book he'll ever write. But, I've heard it really stinks."

Suddenly, it all makes scents. The woman realizes she's in line to see the best-smelling author of the legal thriller *Odor in the Court*.

When the woman gets to the front of the line, she opens her book for the author to sign. "This is so sense-sational!" and she starts to cry with joy.

"Please, let's not get scent-imental," says the skunk.

And with a flick of his pen, he signs her book with his initials:

P.U.

215

TONGUE TWISTER!

Say this fast three times:

The spider got sick after catching a nasty bug.

Q How do ghosts greet each other over coffee?

A "Good mourning to you!"

Q Why did the zombie eat the tightrope walker?

A She wanted a balanced meal.

Q Why did the monster collect scabs?

A It was gross income.

NATE: Have you heard of the boy who uses his bottom to play music?
COCO: No, is he in the school band?
NATE: Yes, he sits in the wind section.

Q What movie did the witch want to see?

A Star Wars.

Q What comes back from the dead and makes honey?

BRAAINS!

A A hive of zom-bees.

BELLA: Where do daddy longlegs hang their stuff?
NOAH: Where?
BELLA: On a-rack-nids.

Q What does a skunk use to watch homemade movies?

A A smell-o-vision.

A lizard sticks its tongue out to smell.

KNOCK, KNOCK.

Who's there?

Mag.

Mag who?

Maggot dinner for all of us. Eat up!

217

KNOCK, KNOCK.

Who's there?
Ooze.
Ooze who?
Ooze coming over besides me?

Frogs secrete a slimy mucus to keep them moist on dry land. Some also use it to thwart predators.

Q What do you call a monster that's covered in boogers?

A A little brother.

Q What do monsters eat for lunch?

A A butt-er and toe-mato manwich.

PADMA: What's worse than encountering a flesh-eating bacteria?
MIRANDA: I have no idea.
PADMA: Summer school.

LAUGHABLE LIST

THE NOT-RECOMMENDED SUMMER READING LIST:

☐ *Fresh Picks* by Iva Bigglebooger

☐ *Going the Distance* by Pat Tooie and Seymour Spitz

☐ *Spontaneous Eruptions* by Di A. Reeya

☐ *What Goes Down Must Come Up: A Physics Lesson* by Barfolomew Yuk

Q Who attended the vampire reunion?

A All the blood relations.

TONGUE TWISTER!

Say this fast three times:

Sally Ander's silly salamander.

Q What did the alligator say when the city mayor condemned his underground home?

A "I'll sewer!"

Q What do you call a monster that smells weird, snores really loud in its sleep, and drools?

A The family dog.

Q Why didn't the dung beetle go to the concert?

A She was too pooped to party.

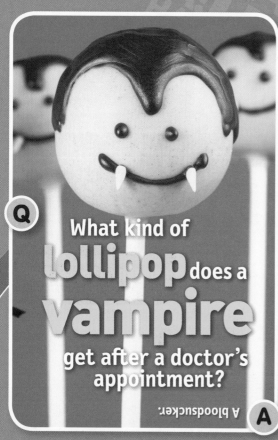

Q What kind of **lollipop** does a **vampire** get after a doctor's appointment?

A A bloodsucker.

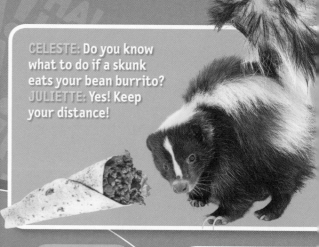

CELESTE: Do you know what to do if a skunk eats your bean burrito?
JULIETTE: Yes! Keep your distance!

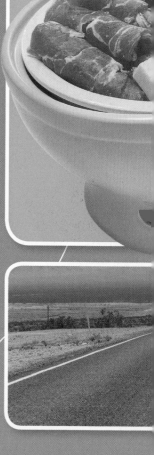

Q What do you call a cat that glows?

A A mew-tant.

pun FUN

Fleas have been **pestering** the **dog** all day.

Q What do you call a monster that has sticky fingers and is afraid of spiders?

A A little sister.

Q Why didn't the woman pass gas at the school assembly?

A She was a private tooter.

Did you know that there is a **restaurant** in Taiwan where food is served in **mini-toilets?**

Toilets also serve as chairs, and the walls are covered in showerheads.

I'M FLUSHED WITH PRIDE!

TAMERA: How did the detective crack the case of the thieving slug?
REGGIE: How?
TAMERA: She followed a trail of ooze.

Q Why did the **fox cross** the road?

A To eat the chicken.

221

KNOCK, KNOCK.

Who's there?

Theodore.
Theodore who?

Theodore is being chewed up by termites.

Sloths are such slow movers that algae grows on their fur.

Q Why don't snakes need to weigh themselves?

A Because they have their own scales.

A ZOMBIE'S BBQ SHOPPING LIST:
☐ Spareribs
☐ Kidney beans
☐ Light bites
☐ Brain juice
☐ Eyes cream

TONGUE TWISTER!

Say this fast three times:

This sushi chef serves serpents.

Q Why did the caterpillar go to France?

A For the Paris-sites.

TREVOR: Which creature gets the most points in a game?
CHASE: I have no clue, tell me.
TREVOR: A score-pion, of course.

STEPHANIE: How did the arachnid know when the girl cheated?
GUS: He had a sixth sense?
STEPHANIE: No, he spider.

Q What did the coach say when the gastropod hit the ball out of the park?

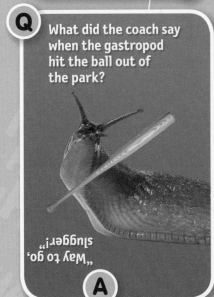

A "Way to go, slugger!"

pun FUN

The zombies went to bed because they were dead tired.

Q What do cats have to wear when they're not litter box trained?

A Dia-purrs.

SOME FISH, such as **herring**, **break wind** to communicate WITH EACH OTHER.

LOL

GROSS

THE ACID in your stomach **can dissolve metal.** NOW THAT'S A BELLY LAUGH!

The **BLOBFISH** HAS **NO** BONES, MUSCLES, OR TEETH.

GIRAFFES sometimes use their **LONG TONGUES** TO CLEAR THEIR EARS AND NOSES.

The largest organism **ON EARTH IS THE "HUMONGOUS FUNGUS."**

BURRRP! EXCUSE ME!

THE **WORLD RECORD** FOR THE LOUDEST BURP IS **LOUDER** THAN A **JACKHAMMER.**

CHAPTER 9

Giggles on the Go

HA!HA!HA!HA!HA!
HA!HA!HA!
HA!HA!
HA!HA!

KNOCK, KNOCK.

Who's there?

Scooter.

Scooter who?

Scooter keys over here and let's take Jenny's bike for a ride.

Scientists provided an exercise wheel in nature for wild mice—and the mice seemed to enjoy running on it, just like pet mice!

Q Why were the cars moving in a row toward the school auditorium?

A They were in an assembly line.

pun FUN

A **locomotive** engineer has **on-the-job** training.

SHANTEL: How did the skeleton cross the river?
MICHELLE: She swam?
SHANTEL: No, she used her scull.

DID YOU SAY TO TURN LEFT OR RIGHT?

Q When is the only time it's okay for an engineer to lose track of a train?

WHAT WAS I ABOUT TO SAY?

A When it's a train of thought.

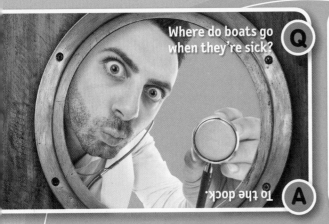

Q Where do boats go when they're sick?

A To the dock.

CARTER: What do captains play on the water?
CECILY: Battleship?
CARTER: No, they play tugboat of war.

Did you know that a bike **traveling** at least eight miles an hour (13 km/h) can keep going **without a rider?**

Bikes are so popular in Amsterdam, in the Netherlands, that there are actually more bikes than people!

TONGUE TWISTER!

Say this fast three times:

Captain Dern, turn the stern to return.

Q What does a pilot say at the end of every day?

A "Biplane!"

Q Why did the choir sign up for a cruise?

A They wanted to hit the high C's together.

231

KATHRYN: Why did the girl speed all the way to the recycling center on her bicycle?
JOSH: I don't know.
KATHRYN: She heard someone shout, "Pedal to the metal!"

Q What does Frankenstein drive?

A A monster truck.

Q How do sand fleas get to the beach?

A On a dune buggy.

YAEL: Let's go for a ride on your bicycle.
DAVE: We can't.
YAEL: Why not?
DAVE: It's two tired.

Q What did the pilot say when she was in a hurry?

A "I've got to jet!"

Q What kind of witchcraft does a witch use to ride a broom?

A Hovercraft.

Q What happened to a member of the Iditarod team when it ran across a slick patch?

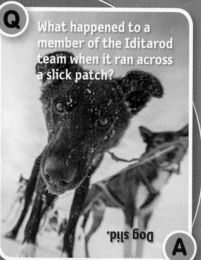

A Dog slid.

Cheetahs are the world's fastest land animals, reaching 70 miles an hour (113 km/h) in just three seconds.

233

KNOCK, KNOCK.

Who's there?
Swan.
Swan who?
Swan to take a boat out on the lake?

Amusement parks around the world have swan-shaped pedal boats.

Q

How does a train conductor decide between two things?

A He choo-choo-chooses one.

Q

Which vehicles get the best TV shows?

A Cable cars.

Q

What do you **call** someone who can **travel** just by touching her **stomach?**

A A belly-porter.

Q

What did the comedian say when the boat captain told a joke?

A "You're ferry funny!"

AKITA: What kind of bandwagon is the most fun to jump on?
PHIL: Hmm ... I don't know.
AKITA: A rubber bandwagon.

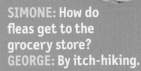

Q

Why was the taxi driver so tired?

A She worked all day without any brakes.

Q

Why did the tourist roll her eyes at the balloon?

A It was full of hot air.

SIMONE: How do fleas get to the grocery store?
GEORGE: By itch-hiking.

235

NAME **Scooter**

FAVORITE ACTIVITY
Hitchhiking

FAVORITE TOY
Tennis ball shaped like a car

PET PEEVE
A flat tire

TRAVELING AT HIGH SPEEDS CAN BE TERRIER-FYING!

I KNEW A DOG WHO CROSSED THE ROAD TO GET TO THE BARKING LOT.

STEP ON THE GAS AND WE'LL SETTER GOOD SPEED.

Plenty of vehicles have been named after animals. They include the Greyhound bus, the Triumph Stag, the Ford Puma, and the Volkswagen Beetle.

pun FUN

Some car races are a total drag.

Why did the boy drag his television into the middle of the street?

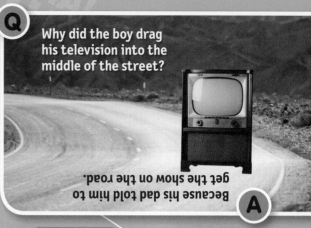

Because his dad told him to get the show on the road.

A

TONGUE TWISTER!

Say this fast three times:

Weld a rear wheel really well.

I'M STARTING TO FEEL DIZZY NOW. . .

JUNE: Did you hear about the girl who blew a giant bubble so she could travel around the world in it?
ELIJAH: No, did it work?
JUNE: Yes, it totally ab-zorb-ed her.

Q Where does Cinderella ride when she flies in an airplane?

A In coach.

Q What's big, sticky, and flies?

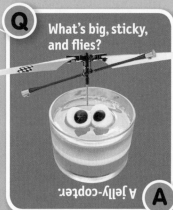

A A jelly-copter.

SUCH POOR STEERING!

Did you know that, in **Kentucky, U.S.A.**, there is a race in which the competitors ride against each other on **ostriches?**

Scientists say that an ostrich's feet are better suited for walking than a human's.

Q

Why did the man stack all his goods on a bike?

A He wanted to pedal his wares.

CODY: What do you call a competition between a sprinter and a train?
SYDNEY: I don't know. What?
CODY: You call it mano a mano-rail.

Q

What did the submarine say to the one next to it?

A "Hey, we're in sink!"

THREE PLANES FILED ONTO THE RUNWAY after a very long day testing out brand-new pilots. "My pilot was impressive," said the first plane to the others. "I think he'll really take off and reach new heights!"

"On my flight a beautiful rainbow came out," said the second plane. "My pilot flew right through it—she definitely passed her test with flying colors." They looked at the third plane and waited to hear his story.

"I had a very long day, too." said the third plane. "My pilot was pretty upset the whole trip."

"What happened?" asked the others.

"He found out his daughter had snuck on board so he grounded her. I don't think he landed the job."

I ALMOST GOT AWAY WITH IT!

KNOCK, KNOCK.

Who's there?
Daris.
Daris who?
Daris room for one more on my snowmobile!

There are 268 species of squirrel, 43 of which can fly. These "flying" squirrels actually glide and can reach distances of 150 feet (46 m).

242

Q What underwater train system do humpbacks take?

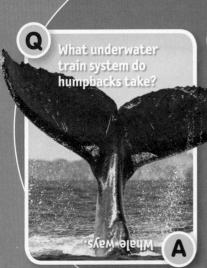

A Whale-ways.

Q What do you call lunch that takes you places in London?

A A double-decker sandwich bus.

Q Where do a fish and a mouse live as roommates?

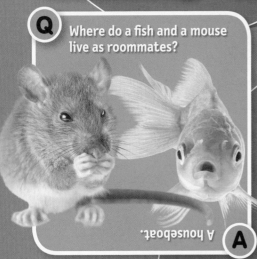

A A houseboat.

Q What kind of public transportation do goblins use?

A Troll-ey buses.

BRAD: A mother called the traffic police to report her seven-year-old son.
STACY: Reported him for what?
BRAD: Driving her up a wall.

Q Why did the man throw his guitar overboard?

A His friends told him not to rock the boat.

Q What did **one oar say to the other?**

A "Canoe help me row to shore?"

JACKIE: What kind of car did dinosaurs drive?
BENNETT: I don't know.
JACKIE: A Model *T. rex*.

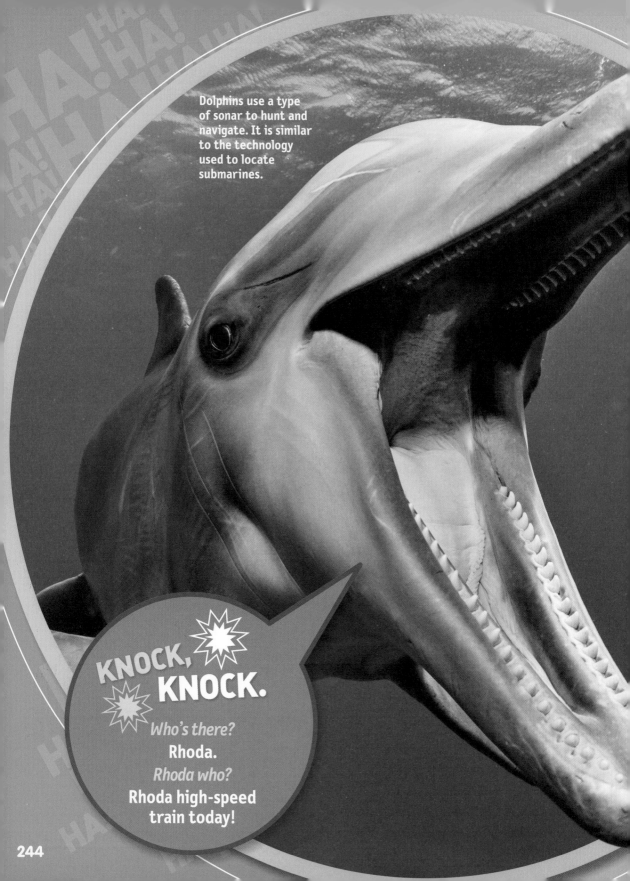

Dolphins use a type of sonar to hunt and navigate. It is similar to the technology used to locate submarines.

KNOCK, KNOCK.

Who's there?
Rhoda.
Rhoda who?
Rhoda high-speed train today!

Q How do bears in the Arctic travel quickly on the ice?

A On polar skates.

Q How did the coast guard get covered in magic glitter?

A They picked up a broken fairy.

Q How do glowworms travel?

A On a light rail.

Q What did the group of sailboats say when the tugboat interrupted them?

A "Way to barge in!"

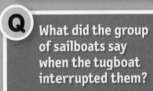

TONGUE TWISTER!

Say this fast three times:

Brock Bach broke Mach ten.

Q What's hairy and used on rivers in Tibet?

A A Ka-yak.

BRAXTON: How do you know that isn't Superman flying above us?
WILLOW: Because it's plane to see.

HA! HA! HA! HA! HA!

KNOCK, KNOCK.

Who's there?
Anita.
Anita who?
Anita lift to school.

Baboons can weigh between 33 and 82 pounds (15 and 37 kg)—about the same as an ocean kayak.

pun FUN

Submarines give me a sinking feeling.

Q Why don't frogs drive cars?

A They always get toad.

Say this fast three times:

"Seize the seas!" says Sneezy Steve.

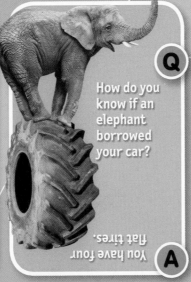

Q How do you know if an elephant borrowed your car?

A You have four flat tires.

LAUGHABLE LIST

SILLY NAMES FOR MONSTER TRUCKS:

- ☐ Tiny Tickler
- ☐ Cupcake Crusher
- ☐ Lil Hugger
- ☐ Daydreamer
- ☐ Cuddle Bunny
- ☐ Mom-mobile

POLICE OFFICER: Sir, do you know why I pulled you over on this one-way street?
MAN: No, I don't. I'm going the right way under the speed limit.
POLICE OFFICER: You weren't speeding, but the right way is driving forward, not in reverse.

Q What kinds of snakes hang out on cars?

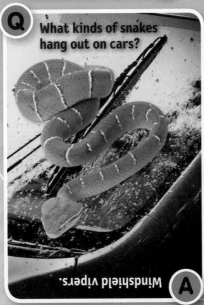

A Windshield vipers.

MARIA: If Bigfoot became president, what would he fly in?
CALEB: I don't know, what?
MARIA: Hair Force One.

NAME **Ollie**

FAVORITE ACTIVITY
**Chasing cats through
the city streets**

FAVORITE TOY
Skateboard

PET PEEVE
Cats on roller skates

YOU CAN'T BEAT THIS FOR WHIZZING AROUND THE CITY. IT'S TRULY MUTT-TROPOLITAN!

THIS IS ONE WAY TO TRAVEL WITHOUT GETTING BOARD.

Bulldogs make great
skateboarders. It
all comes down to
a combination of
size and strength.

249

Q What do vampires drive to get from one island to the next?

A A blood vessel.

Q What kind of flower do car owners like best?

A Carnations.

Q Why did everything on the yacht have price tags on it?

A It was a sale-boat.

Q What did the **soldiers** do after **receiving** a **gift?**

A They sent a tank-you note.

Q What do you need to hear a problem under the hood of a vehicle?

A An engine-ear.

Q What kind of monkeys like to fly?

A Hot-air baboons.

Q What did one electric car say to the other electric car?

A "Hi, Brid!"

New World monkeys like this Ceylon monkey use their tails as a fifth limb to help them travel more swiftly from tree to tree.

KNOCK, KNOCK.

Who's there?

Pat.

Pat who?

Pat-ling is the only way to reach shore with a broken boat motor.

251

LOL ON THE GO

Every year **HOUSTON,** Texas, U.S.A., hosts the **ART CAR PARADE,** which showcases vehicles decorated in **wacky styles,** including a **TACO CAR** and one covered in **TENNIS BALLS.**

BREAK DANCING while wearing roller skates is called **JAM SKATING.**

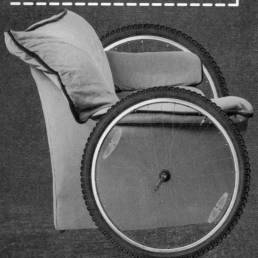

The **COUCHBIKE** combines a **sofa and two bike wheels** so couch potatoes can **PEDAL** around outside without leaving the **COMFORTS** of **HOME.**

I'VE NO HEAD FOR HEIGHTS.

HOT-AIR **BALLOONS** COME IN **SPECIAL SHAPES,** SUCH AS A BULLDOG, A TRACTOR, **A SPACE SHUTTLE,** A T. REX, AND A **CLOWN.**

CHAPTER 10

Jokes You Can Count On

HA!HA!HA!HA!HA!HA!HA!HA!HA!HA!HA!HA!HA!HA!HA!

Q Why is the plus sign happy?

A Because it's always positive.

IZZY: Which country is great at geometry?
THEO: I don't know. Tell me, which?
IZZY: Cube-a!

pun FUN

A calendar **never** takes a **day off.**

I WONDER IF THEY HAVE ANY LOBSTER.

Q How can you tell if a **tree** is good **at math?**

$$\sqrt{4}=2$$

A It has square roots.

Q Why did the circle wink at the triangle?

A Because it thought it was acute.

Q What does a mathematician **bring** to a **picnic?**

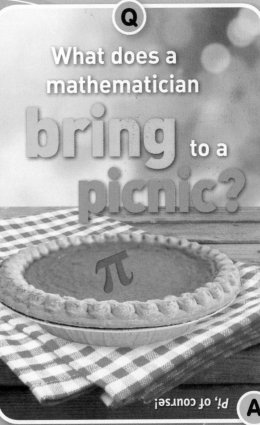

A Pi, of course!

Did you know that the average U.S. **cat owner** spends more than **$1,000** a year on their feline friend?

There are as many as 96 million pet cats in the United States alone!

TONGUE TWISTER!

Say this fast three times:

Sixteen to six things.

DAD: Why did you get an F on your math test?
SON: Because you told me everyone should solve their own problems.
DAD: That's right. And?
SON: I told the teacher he should solve his math problems instead of giving them to me!

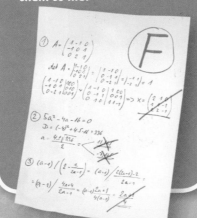

pun FUN

Geometry teachers shouldn't take sides.

Q When did the bank become a circus?

A When it ran out of cents.

Q What did the square say to the circle?

A "Are you going to be a round later?"

Q What did the one say to the seven?

A "I like your hat."

TEACHER: Class, what can you subtract to make seven even?
STUDENT: The s!

Q Why did the math class take a field trip to the beach?

A It was an algae-bra lesson.

KAREEM: Did you hear about the banker who quit his job?
JANE: No, what happened?
KAREEM: He lost interest.

CONFUSED
LOST
PERPLEXED
PUZZLED
UNCLEAR
OFF COURSE

Q What happens when angles crash into each other?

A You get wrecked-angles.

Llama droppings are burned as fuel in Peru.

KNOCK, KNOCK.

Who's there?

Sum.

Sum who?

Sum of us are waiting for you to open the door!

259

KNOCK, KNOCK.

Who's there?
Anita.
Anita who?
**Anita 'nother dime
to make a dollar.**

The panda is an
endangered species.
There are just 1,600
of them living in the
world today.

Q How did the snake get an A in math?

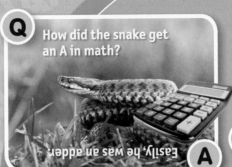

A Easily, he was an adder.

CLARISSA: Which number is most arrogant?
DEIDRE: I don't know.
CLARISSA: The number one, of course, because it's second to none.

Q Why is the **beach** richer than the **mountain?**

A Because the beach has sand dollars.

LAUGHABLE LIST

ON A MATH
TEACHER'S PLAYLIST:

☐ The Jackson 5
☐ One Direction
☐ 5 Seconds of Summer
☐ U2
☐ Four Tops

WALTER: How do you know when a number can't make a decision?
NATASHA: How?
WALTER: When it's having second thoughts.

TONGUE TWISTER!
Say this fast three times:

Brody bought a blue and black bed.

Q Where do numbers go shopping?

A At the deci-mall.

LOU: How did the elephants afford a new car?
HUGH: How?
LOU: They paid peanuts for it.

ETHAN: Where's the sturdiest place to store a number?
AYLA: Where?
ETHAN: In a four-tress.

261

SAY WHAT?

NAME Flipper

FAVORITE ACTIVITY
Flipping coins—heads or tails?

FAVORITE TOY
Fish-shaped calculator

PET PEEVE
Losing count of my catch

ANY LONGER IN THIS ICY WATER AND MY FLIPPERS WILL GO NUMB(ER)!

DO FRESHWATER SEALS KEEP THEIR MONEY AT THE RIVER BANK?

THIS JOKE BOOK GETS MY SEAL OF APPROVAL.

KNOCK, KNOCK.

Who's there?
Nickel.
Nickel who?
Nickel be mad if you don't let him in.

SEALS ARE NOT ALL THAT GOOD AT MATH. THEY ARE BELOW "C" LEVEL IN FACT.

There are 32 species of seal: 18 true seals, nine fur seals, and five sea lions, which include the California sea lion.

Where do math teachers live?

In a subdivision.

A

pun FUN

Never borrow money from elves. They're always short.

Say this fast three times:

Four ferocious felines fear fur.

ENRIQUE: Which part of a house is consistently warm?
AARON: The fireplace?
ENRIQUE: No, the corners. They're always 90 degrees.

$\pi =$

264

Q What do you have when there are

two Elles
in the same
classroom?

A Pair-a-elles.

DANNY: Why couldn't the flamingo pay the taxi fare?
MIKE: Tell me.
DANNY: It only had a one-dollar bill!

THIS IS AN ORCA-STRATED MANEUVER!

Did you know that, for **$100,000**, you can buy a **whale-shaped** submarine?

It can speed along at up to 50 miles an hour (80 km/h).

DOCTOR: You look well-rounded and in shape. What's the problem?
ZERO: I just feel so empty inside.

pun FUN

Only a profit can tell a success from a failure.

Q How many **servings** are in a **pumpkin pie?**

A 3.14.

A DEER WALKED INTO A MEXICAN RESTAURANT.

It ordered five tacos, three burritos, an enchilada combo plate, and a bowl of queso.

The waiter said, "You'll need 30 bucks for that." The deer replied, "Oh, no. This is all for me. I'm starving."

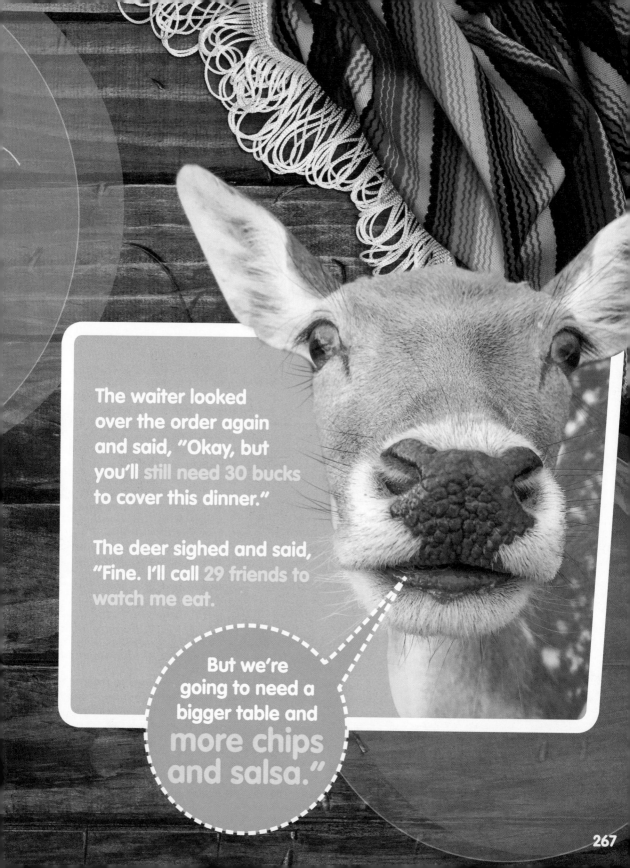

The waiter looked over the order again and said, "Okay, but you'll still need 30 bucks to cover this dinner."

The deer sighed and said, "Fine. I'll call 29 friends to watch me eat.

But we're going to need a bigger table and more chips and salsa."

Say this fast three times:

Eleven elves enliven eleven elephants.

Q How does an army general teach fractions?

A Divide and conquer!

The only solution left is not right.

Q How are bankers like a computer?

A They're always saving.

Q How do you catch a mathematician?

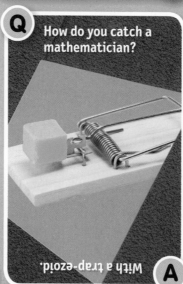

A With a trap-ezoid.

Q What season do numbers like best?

A Sum-mer.

Q What are 3, 5, and 6 called in a snowstorm?

A Numbrrs.

TEACHER: Kayla, you got 10 out of 100 on your quiz. Do you know what you need to do to improve your grade?
KAYLA: Yes. Add a zero to the end.

Q Why did the **accountant** bring a mini model of a **baseball stadium** to the budget meeting?

A The boss had asked for a ballpark figure.

KNOCK, KNOCK.

Who's there?

Bank.

Bank who?

You're welcome, but what are you thanking me for?

An average tiger weighs around 660 pounds (300 kg). That's about the same as eight ten-year-old children.

Orangutans spend as much as 95 percent of their time high up in the treetops of rain forests. They even build their nests up there.

KNOCK, KNOCK.

Who's there?

Juan.

Juan who?

Juan of us is the odd man out.

Q Why did the firefighter hose down the man?

A He said his money was burning a hole in his pocket.

Q Why did the customer pay the baker?

A Because the baker kneaded the dough.

Q Why did the **lady leave** her **table** and **climb** onto the **roof** of the **restaurant?**

A She was told her meal would be on the house.

Q Why was the woman eating money?

A Her friend told her to put her money where her mouth is.

LAUGHABLE LIST

IF IT'S A PARTY OF
ONE AND TWO'S COMPANY AND THREE'S A CROWD, THEN ...

☐ Four is awkwardly standing in the corner.

☐ Five lost the invitation.

☐ Six went to the wrong house.

☐ Seven is feeling lucky because it found five dollars.

CHERYL: Math teachers are scary.
TUCKER: Blood-sucking vampires are scarier.
KEVIN: No, the scariest person is a combination of the two— Count Dracula!

Q What do you call the **shape** that was **knighted?**

A Sir-cle.

Q Why can't one dance with three?

A Because it takes two to tango.

AMANDA: Penny for your thoughts?
JOEL: No way, these things are priceless!

271

Q Where did **3 and 4** go when **they died?**

A They went to seventh heaven.

pun FUN If **7 8 9,** then **10 better run** fast.

NOW THAT'S MILKING IT!

REAGAN: A vampire robbed a bank last week.
YAZMIN: Why?
REAGAN: It was a blood bank.
YAZMIN: Are you sure this story is true?
REAGAN: 0 positive.

Q What do you call a pile of **tangled shoes** that don't have any **matching pairs?**

A The halves and the have knots.

Q Why are computers always rich?

A Because they store a lot of cache.

Q

Why doesn't one trust its neighbor?

A Because he's two-faced.

A dairy cow may produce enough milk in her lifetime to make **9,000 gallons** (34,069 L) of ice cream.

It takes about 350 squirts from a cow's udder to make one gallon (4 L) of milk.

TONGUE 🗣 **TWISTER!**

Say this fast three times:

Surely Sherry shall sell seven seashells.

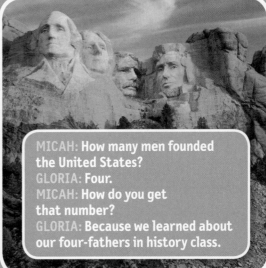

MICAH: How many men founded the United States?
GLORIA: Four.
MICAH: How do you get that number?
GLORIA: Because we learned about our four-fathers in history class.

Q What did the witch love about geometry?

A Hex-agons.

pun FUN

Cheryl had **85 ants** in her ant farm, but when she rounded them up **she had 90.**

NAME Digit

FAVORITE ACTIVITY
Counting my
nine lives

FAVORITE TOY
Mouse pie chart

PET PEEVE
Dogs—they always
zero in on me

ONE, TWO, THREE, FUR, FIVE, SIX, . . .

. . . A CAT THAT COUNTS IS A PRETTY CLAW-SOME CREATURE!

IS THE OPPOSITE OF A NEGATIVE A PAW-SITIVE?

Cats sleep for up
to 15 hours a day.

275

Q Why did the lady take the bank's last dollar bill?

A She thought it was alone.

Q Why were 3 and 5 not hungry when they got together?

A They eight already.

Q What did the zero say to the eight?

A "Cute belt!"

Q What did the referee say to the coin?

A "Catch you on the flip side!"

pun **FUN**

You can **always count on calculators.**

TEAGAN: What kind of cow is very rich?
CASEY: I don't know.
TEAGAN: A cash cow.

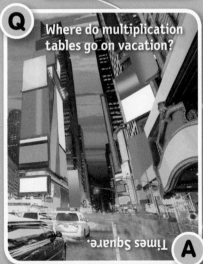

Q How do numbers stay in order?

A With a ruler.

ANDREW: X should buy a compass!
TEACHER: Why?
ANDREW: So we can stop trying to find it!

Q Where do multiplication tables go on vacation?

A Times Square.

A chipmunk's cheek pouches can grow as big as the animal's entire body when full.

KNOCK, KNOCK.

Who's there?

Dozen.

Dozen who?

Dozen anyone know who I am?

There are more than 2,500 species of snake in the world.

Q What did the math teacher say when he found out a shape was missing?

A "Polygon!"

Q Why are math teachers never afraid?

A Because there's safety in numbers.

Q Which fraction is never-ending?

A 24/7.

pun FUN

X is always **missing** because it's a **roamin'** numeral.

JACLYN: You should wear oven gloves when working on circles.
TRISTAN: Why?
JACLYN: Because they are 360 degrees!

MADISON: Are all math problems hard?
KESHA: No, only sum.

Q What did the mountain say to the migrating deer herd?

A "You look like a million bucks."

Q Why are the workers in a clock factory so wealthy?

A They get paid to work overtime every day.

Q What do you call 12 people who are asleep?

A A dozing.

LOL NUMBERS

22 23 24 25 26

A comedian set a **record** by telling **26 JOKES** in ONE MINUTE.

Researchers have identified 19 TYPES OF SMILES.

You are 30 times more likely to LAUGH at something when you're AROUND PEOPLE.

It takes 12 MUSCLES TO SMILE, 11 TO FROWN.

JOKEFINDER

Conversation jokes

Did you know? facts

Knock-knock jokes

Laughable lists

ILLUSTRATIONCREDITS

Credit Abbreviations: SS: Shutterstock; DRMS: Dreamstime; GI: Getty Images; SUS: SuperStock

Front cover:
tr Eric Isselee/SS; cl Rungrujee Meenakanit/SS; br Paul Sutherland/NG
Back cover:
James.Pintar/SS
Spine:
Eric Isselee/SS

1 kuritafsheen/GI; 2tl taboga/SS; 2tc Eric Isselee/SS; 2tr Roman Zaremba/DRMS; 2cl Haveseen/Dreamstime; 2c Mila Atkovska; 2cr DenisNata/SS; 2clb James.Pintar/SS; 2cb starmaro/SS; 2bl James.Pintar/SS; 2br Berendje Photography/SS; 3tr Eric Isselee/SS; 3cl Rungrujee Meenakanit/SS; 3br Paul Sutherland/NG; 4–5 anetapics/SS; 6–7 Alan Dyer/age fotostock/GI; 6–7c alex-mit/iStock/GI; 7cl, c, cr Stramyk/iStock/GI; 8tr Andrey Armyagov/SS; 8tr Maen CG/SS; 8bc ESA, SSC, CXC and STScI/NASA; 8bc Dudarev Mikhail/SS; 9tl Asterixvs/DRMS; 9tr keerati/SS; 8–9c Gordana Sermek/SS; 9cl Yganko/SS; 9bl Jan Schneckenhaus/SS; 9br ESA and G. Bacon (STScI)/NASA; 9br SFerdon/SS; 10tl sashahaltam/SS; 10tc Africa Studio/SS; 10tl Roland IJdema/SS; 10cl ESA and The Hubble Heritage Team (STScI/AURA)/NASA; 10cl Andy Dean Photography/SS; 10cr Lena_graphics/SS; 10cr Elena Schweitzer/SS; 10bl Seaphotoart/SS; 10bc walik/iStock/GI; 10br edobric/SS; 11 Rungrujee Meenakanit/SS;

12 Dudarev Mikhail/SS; 13tc GOLFX/SS; 13tc Darbarti CGI/SS; 13bl Suzanne Tucker/SS; 13bl Eric Isselee/SS; 14–15 DLILLC/Corbis/VCG/GI; 16tc Jurik Peter/SS; 16cl Ronald Sumners/SS; 16cl capitanoseye/SS; 16cr CebotarIN/SS; 16cr IM_photo/SS; 16bl clearviewstock/SS; 16bl Vadim Sadovski/SS; 17tc airdone/SS; 17cl Stephanie Frey/SS; 17cr ESA/Hubble/NASA; 17cr Pavel K/SS; 17bl David Aguilar/NG; 18–19 Anton Jankovoy/SS; 18tr broukoid/SS; 18cl sdominick/iStock/GI; 18br zentilia/SS; 18br Youths/DRMS; 19br egg design/SS; 20 Greg Brave/SS; 21tc Keith Tarrier/SS; 21tc cobalt88/SS; 21tr Fotyma/SS; 21tr Prixel Creative/SS; 21c 3Dsculptor/SS; 21cr Pixel Embargo/SS; 21bl Mega Pixel/SS; 21br Marc Ward/SS; 21br Photodisc; 21br clearviewstock/SS; 22 Anton_Ivanov/SS; 23tc Lena_graphics/SS; 23tc Photobank gallery/SS; 23cl JPL/NASA; 23b glenda/SS; 24tc PRILL/SS; 24cl solarseven/SS; 24cr Dancestrokes/SS; 24–25b Michele Cozzolino/SS; 25tl Brand X; 25tr Aphelleon/SS; 25bc Albert Ziganshin/SS; 25br Coffeemill/SS; 26–27 Only Fabrizio/SS; 28 Panoramic Images/GI; 29tc Linn Currie/SS; 29tc Iakov Kalinin/SS; 29tr AvDe/SS; 29cl Starush/DRMS; 29c NeonLight/SS; 29cr MilousSK/SS; 29bl archy13/SS; 29bl glenda/SS; 29bc angleinast/SS; 30 David Porras/SS; 31tl sumire8/SS; 31cr hideto999/SS; 31bl Vladimir Zadvinskii/SS; 31bl Camille White/SS; 32–33 K Woodgyer/SS; 32tr Fer Gregory/SS; 32cl Praisaeng/SS; 32cl (inset) NASA; 32bc Mcmgraphic/DRMS; 33bl WHITE RABBIT83/SS; 33br lassedesignen/SS; 34–35 Dan Breckwoldt/DRMS; 34–35b Natalia Paklina/SS; 35r Iakov Filimonov/SS; 36tl Pakhnyushchyy/DRMS; 36tl Inara Prusakova/SS; 36tr Panos Karas/SS; 36cl Alan Poulson Photography/SS; 38br Studio DMM Photography, Designs & Art/SS; 38br TTstudio/SS; 37tl Sunny Forest/SS; 37tl Science & Society Picture Library/Contributor/SS; 37tr Kisialiou Yury/SS; 37cr Macrovector/SS; 37cr Nejron Photo/SS; 37bl Kiev.Victor/SS; 37bl exopixel/SS; 37bl pirtuss/SS; 37br Mat Hayward/SS; 38tl Business plus/SS; 38tc R.L.Hausdorf/SS; 38tr meirion matthias/SS; 38cl Valentina_S/SS; 38cl tamaguramo/SS; 38c William Warner/SS; 38cr Bernardbreton/DRMS; 38cr Ivan Ponomarev/SS; 38bl ColoArt/SS; 38bc Brian A Jackson/SS; 38br Martinedegraaf/DRMS; 38br Alexandru Nika/SS; 39 apple2499/SS; 40 Theo Allofs/GI; 41tc Eric Isselee/SS; 41tc Preobrajenskiy/SS; 41cr Glevalex/SS; 41cl Digitalstormcinema/DRMS; 41bl Ivan Ponomarev/SS; 42–43 James.Pintar/SS; 44tl Africa Studio/SS; 44tr pinkomelet/SS; 44cl Perutskyi Petro/SS; 44cl totallypic/SS; 44c Andrey Pavlov/DRMS; 44cr Everett Historical/SS; 44cr Alexandru Nika/SS; 44bl Dorling Kindersley/GI; 44br Fine Art Images/SUS; 45tl Baloncici/SS; 45tr Streluk/DRMS; 45bl Orhan Cam/SS; 45bc goran cakmazovic/SS; 45bc ajt/SS; 45br Sukan-Photo/SS; 45br I. Pilon/SS; 46–47 Yurkoman/SS; 46tr gdvcom/SS; 46tr trekandshoot/SS; 46cr Tanchic/SS; 46cl OZaiachin/SS; 46b Dan Breckwoldt/SS; 47br Sunny studio/SS; 48tr Egor Tetiushev/SS; 48tr Nejron Photo/SS; 48cl Giraphics/SS; 48cl viritphon/SS; 48c gerasimov_foto_174/SS; 48c pick/SS; 48bl Jorge Salcedo/SS; 48bc periscope/SS; 48br SUS; 49 teekayu/SS; 50 Andrew Chin/SS; 51tc Andy Lidstone/SS; 51tc M. Unal Ozmen/SS; 51tr MidoSemsem/SS; 51tr Serg64/SS; 51cl juan carlos tinjaca/SS; 51bl Roxana Bashyrova/SS; 52tr Chardchanin/SS; 52tr Nejron Photo/SS; 52tr karenfoleyphotography/SS; 52cl Geoarts/DRMS; 52cr Dan Breckwoldt/SS; 52cr studio on line/SS; 52–53b jorisvo/SS; 53tl Belenos/SS; 53tl Lakeview Images/SS; 53tr andersphoto/SS; 53tr Peter Lorimer/SS; 53cr Annette Shaff/SS; 53br danjazzia/SS; 54 Edoma/SS; 56tl Chudovska/SS; 56tc japape/SS; 56cl Innocent/DRMS; 56cr Frederic Legrand-COMEO/SS; 56bl Steve Vidler/SS; 56bc bontom/SS; 57 Andrea Izzotti/SS; 58 Sunlight4/DRMS; 59tc Chantal de Bruijne/SS; 59cl Jameswest/DRMS; 59bc Sinisa Botas/SS; 59bl ARTSILENSE/SS; 59bl Rusu Eugen Catalin/DRMS; 60–61 K Woodgyer/SS; 60tl Hurst Photo/SS; 60bl wuviveka/iStock/GI; 60br Tribalium/SS; 61c anekoho/SS; 61t nito/SS; 62–63 S_Photo/SS; 63c Ultrashock/SS; 63ct S_Photo/SS; 62–63b Africa Studio/SS; 64tr yevgeniy11/SS; 64tr Mega Pixel/SS; 64c Ivan_Nikulin/SS; 64cr Carl Stewart/SS; 64b Veronika Surovtseva/SS; 64br photomaster/SS; 65t Andrey_Popov/SS; 65tc Miguel Garcia Saavedra/SS; 65cr Kaneos Media/SS; 65cl little birdie/SS; 65c Kert/SS; 64–65b Maks Narodenko/SS; 65bl Annette Shaff/SS; 65br vchal/SS; 65br blackpixel/SS; 65br Sebastian Enache/SS; 66tl MaraZe/SS; 66tl Babyboom/SS; 66tc espies/SS; 66tr Dan Kosmayer/SS; 66cl timquo/SS; 66c Image Source/GI; 66cr Tiger Images/SS; 66cr Africa Studio/SS; 66bl M. Unal Ozmen/SS; 66 br Vipavlenkoff/SS; 66 br Lev Kropotov/SS; 67 Misja Smits/Buiten-beeld/Minden Pictures/GI; 68 tubuceo/SS; 69tc nito/SS; 69cr Marben/SS; 69cl Ljupco Smokovski/SS; 69cl Danny Smythe/SS; 69br Fabiopagani/DRMS; 69bl M. Unal Ozmen/SS; 70–71 Gary Vestal/GI; 72tr RoongsaK/SS; 72tr Ivonne Wierink/SS; 72cl Denis Larkin/SS; 72cr Brenda Carson/SS; 72cr M. Cornelius/SS; 72bl margouillat photo/SS; 72bc Space Monkey Pics/SS; 73tr Javier Brosch/SS; 73c Melica/SS; 73cr urfin/SS; 73bl photovs/SS; 73bl Brian McEntire/SS; 73br Pressmaster/SS; 74–75 M. Unal Ozmen/SS; 74tr Christopher Elwell/SS; 75bl Gregory Johnston/SS; 75r Jason Miller/GI; 76tl KuKanDo/SS; 76tc Daniel Prudek/SS; 76tr Tommy Alven/SS; 76c Binh Thanh Bui/SS; 76c Azuzl/SS; 76cr Dasha Petrenko/SS; 76bl Jose Ramon Cagigas/SS; 76bl wk1003mike/SS; 76bc LIUSHENGFILM/SS; 76bc Africa Studio/SS; 76br Ines Behrens-Kunkel/SS; 76br Hong Vo/SS; 77 Ger Bosma/GI; 78 bearerofchrist/iStock/GI; 79tc Vector Tradition SM/SS; 79tc Pavel Savchuk/SS; 79tc Binh Thanh Bui/SS; 79cl Mantana Boonsatr/SS; 79cr Kostenyukova Nataliya/SS; 79cr chrisbrignell/SS; 79bl Tyler Olson/SS; 79br DronG/SS; 80tl artjazz/SS; 80tl Africa Studio/SS; 80cl a454/SS; 80cl Danny Smythe/SS; 80–81c zhengzaishuru/SS; 80–81c Designsstock/SS; 80–81bc Africa Studio/SS; 81tl WilleeCole Photography/SS; 81tr stockcreations/SS; 81bc Binh Thanh Bui/SS; 81bc Nastya22/SS; 81br Africa Studio/SS; 81br visivastudio/SS; 82–83 photomaster/SS; 84tl Zurijeta/SS; 84cr Drakuliren/SS; 84cr orriPhoto/SS; 84cl Olga_sweet/DRMS; 84cl Robyn Mackenzie/SS; 84c zkruger/SS; 84bc Gvictoria/SS; 84bc Maks Narodenko/SS; 85 Holger Leue/GI; 86 Steven Skelly/EyeEm/GI; 87tc Duncan Andison/SS; 87tc bkp/SS; 87c avlo_K/SS; 87cr wavebreakmedia/SS; 87br M. Unal Ozmen/SS; 88–89 K Woodgyer/SS; 88tr SvetPavlova/SS; 88cl lazyllama/SS; 88cl A_M_Radul/SS; 88br Everett Collection/SS; 88br Arcady/SS; 89tl Javier Brosch/SS; 89tlb kittipong053/SS; 89cl Davydenko Yuliia/SS; 89clb Sheila Fitzgerald/SS; 89bl Pixfiction/SS; 89tr larryrains/SS; 90–91 Ken Backer/DRMS; 91tl Smiltena/SS; 91tc Stefano Raffini/iStock/GI; 91tc Olga Vasilek/SS; 91cl Kevkhiev Yury/DRMS; 91cl Elnur/SS; 92tr concept w/SS; 92cl glenda/SS; 92bl Rich Carey/SS; 92br Triocean/SS; 93tl Sascha Burkard/SS; 93tl DutchScenery/SS; 93cr Richard Whitcombe/SS; 93cl Eric Isselee/SS; 93crb Evikka/SS; 93br sainthorant daniel/SS; 94tl nicobatista/SS; 94tl Vladyslav Starozhylov/SS; 94tc farres/SS; 94tr s-ts/SS; 94cl Gang Liu/SS; 94c humbak/SS; 94cr Africa Studio/SS; 94bl Ilya Akinshin/SS; 94bl Dan Kosmayer/SS; 94br Fer Gregory/SS; 95 Karine Aigner/GI; 96 Robert Mooney/GI; 97tr Sashkin/SS; 97cr Vorobyeva/SS; 97br leungchopan/SS; 97br Juriah Mosin/SS; 97bl Kameel4u/DRMS; 98–99 Eric Isselee/SS; 100t Sudpoth Sirirattanasakul/SS; 100cl posteriori/SS; 100cl Warongdech/SS; 100clb VGstockstudio/SS; 100cr Martin Prochazkacz/SS; 100bl exopixel/SS; 101tr VGstockstudio/SS; 101cr Mega Pixel/SS; 101b A StockStudio/SS; 102–103 Annette Shaff/SS; 102tr antpkr/SS; 102bl Jim Barber/SS; 103 WilleeCole Photography/SS; 104 Radka Tesarova/SS; 105tc KPG_Payless/SS; 105tr Marek Szumlas/SS; 105c Javier Brosch/SS; 105c Bryan Solomon/SS; 105cr kongsak sumano/SS; 105bl Janis Smits/SS; 105br Mikesilent/SS; 106 Doty911/SS; 107tc Caravana/DRMS; 107cr arka38/SS; 107bl Andrey Lobachev/SS; 108tl XiXinXing/SS; 108tr holbox/SS; 108cl Dim Dimich/SS; 108cl Thomas Brain/SS; 108cl Pferd/SS; 108cr Denise Kappa/SS; 108br Lehrer/SS; 109tl Chris Hill/SS; 109tr James Steidl/SS; 109tr Pixfiction/SS; 109cr Kalmatsuy/SS; 109br tobkatrina/SS; 110–111 Adrizon/DRMS; 112 Christian Heinrich/GI; 113tl mikeledray/SS; 113tc underworld/SS; 113tr Praisaeng/SS; 113tr Sanit Fuangnakhon/SS; 113bl dtopal/SS; 113cr winnond/SS; 113bl wavebreakmedia/SS; 113bc alina_veronika/SS; 114 Picture by Tambako the Jaguar/GI; 115tr graphic stocker/SS; 115tr Artieskg/SS; 115cr Alfred Gruener/SS; 115cr Dimedrol68/SS; 115bl Kostsov/SS; 115bl 5/SS; 115br tomertu/SS; 116–117 K Woodgyer/SS; 116tr photosync/SS; 116cl WilleeCole Photography/SS; 116br Sebastian Kaulitzki/SS; 116br AF studio/SS; 117l Andrey Armyagov/SS; 117tr benchart/SS; 118–119 Rob Lewine/GI; 118–119 Millisenta/SS; 119l Ermolaev Alexander/SS; 120tl CREATISTA/SS; 120tc Sergey Nivens/SS; 120c Vladimir Gjorgiev/SS; 120br the palms/SS; 120br vipman/SS; 121tl dien/SS; 121tl erraceStudio/SS; 121tr Photoonlife/SS; 121cr jcrosemann/SS; 121br Avesun/SS; 121br Michal Ludwiczak/SS; 122tl Gudkov Andrey/SS; 122tr R. Gino Santa Maria/Shutterfree, Llc/DRMS; 122cl Everett Historical/SS; 122c Thomas Marent/Minden Pictures/SUS; 122cl Blue Planet Earth/SS; 122br Vania Georgieva/SS; 123 Steve Vidler/SS; 124 Robert McGouey/All Canada Photos/SUS; 125tc kirill_makarov/SS; 125tr Minerva Studio/SS; 125cl Harvepino/SS; 125cr 5 second Studio/SS; 125bl Tsekhmister/DRMS; 126l VVCephei/iStock/GI; 126–127 Mark Thiessen/NG; 127c vaschenko Roman/SS; 128tl Georgios Kollidas/SS; 128tl abiru/SS; 128tr Africa Studio/SS; 128cl Siede Preis/GI; 128cl 1000 Words/SS; 128–129b Flashon/DRMS; 129tl Oliver Hoffmann/SS; 129tr SoisudaS/SS; 129cr Karen Struthers/SS; 129br rangizzz/SS; 129br Anneka/SS; 130–131 B Brown/SS; 130tr artjazz/SS; 130bl Robynrg/SS; 131c Rebecca Hale/NG; 132 Tobias Friedrich/F1 ONLINE/SUS; 133tl Ollyy/SS; 131tr Valentyna Chukhlyebova/SS; 133cl neelsky/SS; 133cl avian/SS; 133c italianestro/SS; 133cr SUS; 133bc Quality Stock Arts/SS; 133br Miles Davies/SS; 134 Minden Pictures/SUS; 135tc Lindsay Helms/SS; 135cr Elena Schweitzer/SS; 135cl Photographerlondon/DRMS; 135bl Mega Pixel/SS; 135bl Africa Studio/SS; 136tl Eric Isselee/SS; 136tc zimmytws/SS; 136tr Africa Studio/SS; 136cl Transia Design/SS; 136c kirill_makarov/SS; 136–137c charles taylor/SS; 136bc vengerof/SS; 137t AlexussK/SS; 137c valdis torms/SS; 137cr Gustavo Frazao/SS; 137cr vladwel/SS; 136–137b Fer Gregory/SS; 136–137b anfisa focusova/SS; 138–139 nattanan726/SS; 140tc Fireflyphoto/DRMS; 140tr Misunseo/SS; 140cl Lorna/DRMS; 140cr Boris Sosnovyy/SS; 140bl Rosa Jay/SS; 140br Ociacia/SS; 141 Barrett Hedges/Getty Images; 142 Javier Brosch/SS; 143tl LifetimeStock/SS; 143cr Rrraum/SS; 143bl yakub88/SS; 144–145 K Woodgyer/SS; 144tr Shcherbakov Ilya/SS; 144tr Richard Thomas/DRMS; 144tr vector_brothers/SS; 144cl Jagodka/SS; 144b John Lund/Stephanie Roeser/GI; 145c SmileStudio/SS; 145b Bilal Shafi/SS; 146–147 Egon Zitter/DRMS; 146–147c Seaphototoart/DRMS; 147br Eduardo Rivero/SS; 147br ded pixto/SS; 148tl Shahril KHMD/SS; 148tc stuart.ford/SS; 148cl eurobanks/SS; 148–149c Corey Hayes/GI; 148–149b Christian

Published by National Geographic Partners, LLC.
All rights reserved. Reproduction of the whole or any part of
the contents without written permission from the publisher
is prohibited.

Since 1888, the National Geographic Society has funded more
than 12,000 research, exploration, and preservation projects
around the world. The Society receives funds from National
Geographic Partners, LLC, funded in part by your purchase.
A portion of the proceeds from this book supports this vital
work. To learn more, visit natgeo.com/info.

NATIONAL GEOGRAPHIC and Yellow Border Design are
trademarks of the National Geographic Society, used
under license.

For more information, visit nationalgeographic.com,
call 1-800-647-5463, or write to the following address:

National Geographic Partners
1145 17th Street N.W.
Washington, D.C. 20036-4688 U.S.A.

Visit us online at nationalgeographic.com/books

For librarians and teachers: ngchildrensbooks.org

More for kids from National Geographic:
kids.nationalgeographic.com

For information about special discounts for bulk
purchases, please contact National Geographic Books
Special Sales: specialsales@natgeo.com

For rights or permissions inquiries, please contact
National Geographic Books Subsidiary Rights:
bookrights@natgeo.com

Design, Editorial, and Production by
Toucan Books, LTD

Trade paperback ISBN: 978-1-4263-2879-4
Reinforced library binding ISBN: 978-1-4263-2880-0

Printed in China
17/RRDS/1

The publisher would like to thank the following people for
making this book possible. At National Geographic: Kate
Hale, senior editor; Callie Broaddus, senior designer; Sarah
J. Mock, senior photo editor; Paige Towler, associate editor;
Joan Gossett, editorial production manager; Molly Reid,
production editor; and Anne LeongSon and Gus Tello, design
production assistants. At Toucan Books, Ltd: Anna Southgate,
editor; Lee Riches, designer; Helvi Cranfield, Kris Hanneman,
and Sharon Southren, picture research; Marion Dent, proof-
reader; and Urusla Caffrey, indexer.